A Handbook of Basic Law Terms

BRYAN A. GARNER
Editor

DAVID W. SCHULTZ
LANCE A. COOPER
STEPHEN W. KOTARA
Assistant Editors

WEST
GROUP

St. Paul, Minnesota
1999

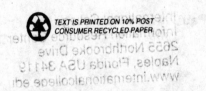

PREFACE

There are many things that educated people are expected to know something about. But when it comes to relative importance, few of those things can rival the law, which affects almost every aspect of modern life. The problem for those wishing to learn about law is that, as society grows more complex by the year, so does our law. And for some, it's tempting to give up trying to understand anything as complex as American law.

If you want to resist this temptation—and I hope you do—you'll need some guidance. That's where this book comes in. It might be called a dictionary of legal literacy: it contains the most important and most common words and phrases used in law. These terms denote fundamental legal concepts. And learning the vocabulary is an excellent start in learning about any discipline.

Whether you use this *Handbook* as a vocabulary-builder or as a quick reference, my colleagues and I hope you'll find it helpful.

BRYAN A. GARNER

Dallas, Texas
November 1998

*

CONTENTS

*

A

abandonment. 1. The act of giving up some right or interest with the intent of never claiming it again. **2.** In family law, the act of leaving a spouse or children willfully and without an intent to return.

abet, *vb.* **1.** To encourage and assist (someone), esp. in the commission of a crime <abet a known felon>. **2.** To support (a crime) by active assistance <abet a robbery>. See AID AND ABET.

abstention. A federal court's relinquishment of jurisdiction over a case to avoid needless conflict with a state's administration of its own affairs.

abstract of judgment. A copy or summary of a judgment that, when filed with the appropriate public office, creates a lien on the judgment debtor's nonexempt property.

abstract of title. A concise statement, usu. prepared for a mortgagee or purchaser of real property, summarizing the history of a piece of land, including all conveyances, interests, liens, and encumbrances that affect title to the land.

abuse of discretion. **1.** A judge's failure to exercise sound, reasonable, and legal decision-making. **2.** An appellate court's standard for reviewing a lower court's decision that is asserted to be grossly unsound, unreasonable, or illegal. See DISCRETION.

acceleration clause. A loan-agreement provision requiring the debtor to pay off the balance sooner than the regular payment date if some specified event occurs, such as failure to timely pay installments or to maintain insurance.

acceptance. An agreement, either by express act or by implication from conduct, to the terms of an offer so that a binding contract is formed. ● If an acceptance modifies the offer's terms or adds new ones, it usu. operates as a counteroffer. See OFFER.

accessory. A person who aids or contributes in the commission of a crime. ● An accessory is usu. liable only if the crime is a felony. Cf. PRINCIPAL (2).

accomplice. A person who voluntarily and intentionally participates with another in committing a crime and thus becomes punishable for it.

accord and satisfaction. An agreement to substitute for an existing debt some alternative form of discharging that debt, coupled with the actual discharge of the debt by the substituted performance. ● The new agreement is called the *accord*, and the discharge is called the *satisfaction*.

accusation. **1.** A formal charge of criminal wrongdoing. ● The accusation is usu. presented to a court or magistrate having jurisdiction to inquire into the alleged crime. **2.** An informal statement that a person has engaged in an illegal or wrongful act.

accused, *n.* A person whom someone has blamed of wrongdoing <the police officer questioned the accused>.

acknowledgment. **1.** A formal declaration made in the presence of an authorized officer, such as a notary public, by someone who signs a document and says that the signature is authentic. Cf. VERIFICATION (1). **2.** The officer's certificate that is affixed to the document.— Also termed (in sense 2) *certificate of acknowledgment*.

acquittal. In criminal law, the legal certification, usu. by jury verdict, that an accused person is not guilty of the charged offense.

3

action. A civil or criminal judicial proceeding.

act of God. An overwhelming, unpreventable event caused exclusively by forces of nature, such as an earthquake, flood, or tornado. Cf. FORCE MAJEURE.

actual authority. Authority that a principal intentionally confers on an agent, including the authority that the agent reasonably believes he or she has as a result of the agent's dealings with the principal. ● Actual authority can be either express or implied. Cf. APPARENT AUTHORITY.

actual damages. A monetary amount awarded to a complainant to compensate for a proven injury or loss; damages that repay actual losses.—Also termed *compensatory damages*.

actual notice. Notice given to a party directly or presumed to be received personally because the evidence within the party's knowledge is sufficient to put him or her on inquiry. Cf. CONSTRUCTIVE NOTICE.

actus reus (**ak**-təs-**ray**-əs *or* -**ree**-). [Law Latin "guilty act"] The wrongful deed that comprises the physical components of a crime and that generally must be coupled with *mens rea* to establish criminal liability <the *actus reus*

4

for murder is killing another person>. Cf. MENS REA.

adhesion contract. A standard-form contract prepared by one party, to be signed by the party in a weaker position (usu. a consumer) who has little choice about the terms.

adjudication (ə-joo-di-**kay**-shən). **1.** The legal process of resolving a dispute; the process of judicially deciding a case. **2.** JUDGMENT.

ad litem (ad-lɪ-təm). [Latin "for the suit"] For the purposes of the suit; pending the suit. See GUARDIAN AD LITEM.

administration. The management and settlement of the estate of an intestate decedent, or of a testator who has no executor, by a person (an *administrator*) appointed and supervised by the court.

administrative law. The law governing the organization and operation of the executive branch of government (including independent agencies) and the relations of the executive with the legislature, the judiciary, and the public. • Administrative law primarily concerns agency rulemaking and investigations.

administrator. A person appointed by the court to manage the assets and liabilities of an intestate decedent or of a testator who has no executor. Cf. EXECUTOR.

admiralty. 1. A court that exercises jurisdiction over all maritime contracts, torts, injuries, or offenses.—Also termed *admiralty court*; *maritime court*. **2.** The jurisprudence that has grown out of the practice of admiralty courts. **3.** Narrowly, the rules governing contract, tort, and workers'-compensation claims arising out of commerce on or over water.—Also termed (in senses 2 & 3) *admiralty law*. See MARITIME LAW.

admissible, *adj.* Allowable; permissible <the blood samples were admissible as evidence>.

adoption. 1. In family law, the statutory process of terminating a child's legal rights and duties toward the natural parents and substituting similar rights and duties toward adoptive parents. **2.** In contract law, the process by which a person agrees to assume a contract that was previously made for that person's benefit, such as a newly formed corporation's acceptance of a preincorporation contract.

ADR. *abbr.* ALTERNATIVE DISPUTE RESOLUTION.

ad valorem tax. A tax imposed proportionally on the value of something (esp. real property), rather than on its quantity.

adversary system. A procedural system, such as the Anglo–American legal system, involving active and unhindered parties contesting with each other to present a case to an independent decision-maker.

adverse possession. A method of acquiring title to real property by possessing it for a statutory period under certain conditions, esp. by a nonpermissive use of the property with a claim of right when that use is continuous, exclusive, hostile, open, and notorious. Cf. PRE-SCRIPTION.

affiant (ə-fı-ənt). A person who swears to the facts declared in an affidavit.

affidavit. A voluntary declaration of facts written down and sworn to by the affiant before an officer authorized to administer oaths <the lawyer drafted the affidavit for the client to review and sign>. ● A great deal of evidence is submitted by affidavit, esp. in pre-trial matters such as summary-judgment motions.

affirm, *vb.* **1.** To approve (a lower court's decision); to confirm or ratify <the trial court's judgment was affirmed on appeal>. Cf. REVERSE. **2.** To pledge the truth of something in lieu of making an oath; to make an affirmation

<the witness affirmed that he was at home during the robbery>.

affirmation. A pledge equivalent to an oath but without reference to a supreme being or to "swearing." ● While an oath is "sworn to," an affirmation is merely "affirmed," but either type of pledge may subject the person making it to prosecution for perjury. Cf. OATH.

affirmative defense. A defense raising new facts and arguments that, if true, will defeat the plaintiff's or prosecution's claim even if all allegations in the complaint are true. ● Examples of affirmative defenses include duress and contributory negligence (in civil cases) and insanity and self-defense (in criminal cases).

agency. A fiduciary relationship created by express or implied contract or by law, in which one party (the *agent*) may act on behalf of another party (the *principal*) and bind that other party by words or actions.

agent. One who is authorized to act for or in place of another; a representative <a professional football player's agent>. Cf. PRINCIPAL (1); EMPLOYEE.

aggravated, *adj.* (Of a crime) made worse or more serious by circumstances such as violence, the presence of a deadly weapon, or the intent to commit another crime <aggravated robbery>.

aid and abet, *vb.* To assist or facilitate the commission of a crime, or to promote its accomplishment. ● Aiding and abetting is a crime in most states.

alibi. A defense of having been at a place other than the scene of the crime <Fred's alibi was that he was out of the country when the robbery occurred>.

alien. A person who resides within the borders of a country but is not a citizen or subject of that country; a person not owing allegiance to a particular nation. ● In the United States, an alien is a person who is born outside the country, who is subject to some foreign government, and who has not been granted citizenship under U.S. law.

alienation. Conveyance or transfer of property to another <alienation of one's land>.

alimony. A court-ordered allowance that one spouse pays to the other spouse for maintenance and support while they are separated, while their divorce is pending, or after they are divorced.—Also termed *spousal support*; *maintenance.* Cf. CHILD SUPPORT.

allegation. Something declared or asserted as a matter of fact, esp. in a legal pleading; a party's formal statement of a factual matter as being true or provable, without it yet having been proved <the allegation in the complaint was that the plaintiff slipped on a wet floor>.

alter ego. A corporation used by an individual in conducting personal business, such that a court may impose personal liability on the individual by piercing the corporate veil when fraud has been perpetrated on someone dealing with the corporation <Sims sued both Mack and Mack's company because he claimed that the company was Mack's alter ego>. See PIERCING THE CORPORATE VEIL.

alternative dispute resolution. A procedure for settling a dispute by means other than litigation, such as arbitration or mediation.—Abbr. ADR.

amended pleading. A pleading that replaces an earlier pleading and that contains matters omitted from or not known at the time of the earlier pleading. Cf. SUPPLEMENTAL PLEADING.

amicus curiae (ə-**mee**-kəs-**k[y]oor**-ee-ı *or* **am**-i-kəs -*or* ə-**mı**-kəs). [Latin "friend of the court"] A person who is not a party to a lawsuit but who petitions the court to file a

10

brief in the action because that person has a strong interest in the subject matter.—Often shortened to *amicus*.—Also termed *friend of the court*. Pl. **amici curiae.**

annotation. 1. A brief summary of the facts and decision in a case, esp. one involving statutory interpretation. **2.** A note that explains or criticizes (usu. a case), esp. to give, in condensed form, some indication of the law as deduced from cases and statutes, as well as to point out where similar cases can be found. • Annotations appear, for example, in the *United States Code Annotated* (U.S.C.A.).

annuity. 1. An obligation to pay a stated sum, usu. monthly or annually, to a stated recipient. • These payments terminate upon the death of the designated beneficiary. **2.** A fixed sum of money payable periodically.

annulment. A judicial or ecclesiastical declaration that a marriage is void. • Unlike a divorce, an annulment establishes that marital status never existed.

answer, *n.* In civil procedure, a defendant's first pleading that addresses the merits of the case, usu. by denying the plaintiff's allegations and setting forth any defenses. Cf. COMPLAINT (1).

anticipatory repudiation. Rejection or renunciation of a contractual duty before the time for performance, giving the injured party an immediate right to damages for total breach, as well as discharging the injured party's remaining duties of performance.

antitrust law. The body of law designed to protect trade and commerce from restraints, monopolies, price-fixing, and price discrimination. ● The principal federal antitrust statutes are the Sherman Act (15 U.S.C.A. §§ 1–7) and the Clayton Act (15 U.S.C.A. §§ 12–27).

apparent authority. Authority that a third party reasonably believes an agent has, based on the third party's dealings with the principal. ● Apparent authority can be created by law even when no actual authority has been conferred. Cf. ACTUAL AUTHORITY.

appeal, *n.* A proceeding undertaken to reverse a decision by bringing it to a higher authority; esp., the submission of a lower court's or agency's decision to a higher court for review and possible reversal <Paula thought she had a good chance to win on appeal>.

appearance. A coming into court as a party or interested person, or as a lawyer on behalf

of a party or interested person <Judy's lawyer filed an appearance as her counsel of record>.

appellant (ə-**pel**-ənt). A party who appeals a lower court's decision, usu. seeking reversal of that decision.

appellate court. A court with jurisdiction to review decisions of one or more lower courts.

appellate review. Examination of a lower court's decision by a higher court, which can affirm, reverse, or modify the decision.

appellee (ap-ə-**lee**). A party against whom an appeal is taken and whose role is to respond to that appeal, usu. by urging affirmance of the lower court's decision.

arbitration. A method of dispute resolution involving one or more neutral third parties who are agreed to by the disputing parties and whose decision is binding. Cf. MEDIATION.

arm's-length, *adj.* Of or relating to dealings between two parties who are not related or not on close terms and who are presumed to have roughly equal bargaining power <the CEO's service contract with his daughter's mainte-nance company was not an arm's-length trans-action>.

arraignment. In a criminal prosecution, the initial proceeding in which the defendant is brought before the court to hear the charges and enter a plea.

array. See VENIRE.

arrest, *n.* The taking or keeping of a person in custody by legal authority, esp. in response to a criminal charge.

arrest warrant. A warrant, issued only on probable cause, directing a law-enforcement officer to arrest a person and to bring that person to court. Cf. SEARCH WARRANT.

arson. The crime of intentionally burning someone else's property (as to destroy a building) or one's own property (as to collect insurance).

articles of incorporation. The document that legally creates a corporation when filed with the appropriate governmental agency, usu. the secretary of state. ● The articles typically establish the corporation's purpose and duration, the rights and liabilities of shareholders and directors, and the classes of stock and other securities. Cf. CHARTER (2).

as is. In the existing condition without modification <the buyer bought the used car as is>.

● Under the UCC, a seller can disclaim all implied warranties by stating that the goods are being sold "as is" or "with all faults."

assault, *n.* **1.** In criminal law and tort law, the threat or use of force that causes the victim to have a reasonable apprehension of imminent harmful or offensive contact. **2.** In criminal law only, an attempt to commit battery, requiring the specific intent to cause physical injury. **3.** Loosely, a criminal battery. Cf. BATTERY.

assignee (as-ə-**nee** *or* ə-**sın**-ee). One to whom property rights or powers are transferred by another.—Also termed *assign.*

assignment. 1. The transfer of rights or property; the rights or property so transferred <assignment of royalty interests>. **2.** The instrument of transfer <Louis attested the assignment before a notary public>.

assignor (as-ə-**nor** *or* ə-**sın**-ər). One who transfers property rights or powers to another.—Also spelled *assigner.*

assumption of the risk. 1. The act or an instance of a prospective plaintiff's taking on the risk of loss or injury <the skydiver's assumption of the risk>. **2.** In tort law, the principle that a person who has taken on the risk of loss or injury cannot maintain an action against the party who caused the loss or injury <the judge instructed the jury not to consider assumption of the risk as a defense>. ● Assumption of the risk was originally an affirmative defense, but in most states it has now been subsumed within the doctrines of contributory negligence or comparative negligence.

attachment. The seizure or taking control of a person's property esp. to satisfy a judgment against the person. Cf. GARNISHMENT; SEQUESTRATION (1).

attempt, *n.* In criminal law, an overt act that is done with the intent to commit a crime but that falls short of completing the crime. ● Attempt is a separate offense from the attempted crime.

attest, *vb.* **1.** To bear witness; testify <Susan attested that the defendant was with her on the night of the burglary>. **2.** To affirm to be true or genuine; to authenticate by signing as a witness <Edward attested the codicil to the will>.

attorney. 1. Strictly, one who is designated to transact business for another; a legal agent.— Also termed *attorney-in-fact.* **2.** A person who practices law; a lawyer.—Also termed (in sense 2) *attorney-at-law*.

attorney-client privilege. A client's right to refuse to disclose and to prevent any other person from disclosing confidential communications between the client and his or her attorney.

attorney-in-fact. See ATTORNEY (1).

attractive nuisance. A dangerous condition that may attract children onto land, thus causing a risk to their safety <the concrete company's sandpile was an attractive nuisance>.

at will. Of or relating to a legal relationship that continues until either party wishes to terminate it <tenancy at will> <at-will employee>.

authentication. The act of proving that something (usu. a document) is true or genuine, esp. so that it may be admitted as evidence; the condition of being so proved <authentication of the medical records>.

authority. 1. The right or permission to legally act on another's behalf; the power delegated by a principal to an agent <authority to sign the contract>. See AGENCY. **2.** Governmental power or jurisdiction <the search was within

the police officer's authority>. **3.** A governmental agency or corporation that administers a public enterprise <housing authority>. **4.** A legal writing taken as definitive or decisive; esp., a judicial or administrative decision cited as a precedent <that opinion is good authority in Idaho>. **5.** A source, such as a statute, case, or treatise, cited in support of a legal argument <the brief cited several authorities>.

automatic stay. In bankruptcy, a bar to all judicial or extrajudicial collection efforts against the debtor or the debtor's property <the automatic stay prevented the creditor from repossessing Jeff's car>. ● The automatic stay takes effect as soon as the bankruptcy petition is filed, but it applies only to debts incurred before the filing.

award, *n.* A final judgment or decision, esp. one by a jury or arbitrator assessing damages.

B

bad faith. **1.** Dishonesty of belief or purpose <the lawyer filed the pleading in bad faith>. **2.** An insurance company's unreasonable and unfounded (though not necessarily fraudulent) refusal to provide coverage <the insurer's decision not to pay for the roof damage was bad faith>. **3.** An insured's claim against an insurance company for an unreasonable and unfounded refusal to provide coverage <Cox sued the insurance company for bad faith and breach of contract>. Cf. GOOD FAITH.

bail, *n.* **1.** A security such as cash or a bond; esp., security required by a court for the release of a prisoner who must appear at a future time <the judge set bail at $5,000>. **2.** Release of a prisoner on security for a future appearance <Dixon was ordered to stay within the city limits while free on bail>.

bailee. One to whom personal property is delivered as a bailment. ● A bailee is usu. hired to store or transport goods.

bailiff. A court officer who maintains order among the parties, attorneys, and jury during court proceedings.

bailment. **1.** A delivery of personal property by one person (the *bailor*) to another (the *bailee*) who holds the property under an express or implied-in-fact contract. ● Unlike a sale or gift of personal property, a bailment involves a change in possession but not in title. **2.** The personal property delivered by the bailor to the bailee.

bailor. One who delivers personal property to another as a bailment.

bankruptcy. The statutory procedure, usu. triggered by insolvency, by which a person is relieved of most debts and undergoes a judicially supervised reorganization or liquidation for the benefit of that person's creditors. See INSOLVENCY.

bar, *n.* **1.** The whole body of lawyers qualified to practice in a given court or jurisdiction; the legal profession, or an organized subset of it <the state bar can discipline its members>. **2.** A particular court or system of courts <the case at bar is unique>. **3.** A preventive barrier to or the destruction of a legal action or claim; the effect of a judgment for the defendant <the jury's verdict was a bar to any further lawsuits>.

barratry (**bair**-ə-tree *or* **bar**-). Vexatious persistence in, or incitement to, litigation. ● Barratry is a crime in most states.

battery. 1. In criminal law, the application of force to another resulting in harmful or offensive contact. ● Battery is a misdemeanor under most modern statutes. **2.** In tort law, an intentional and offensive touching of another. Cf. ASSAULT.

bearer. A person who possesses a negotiable instrument marked "payable to bearer" or indorsed in blank.

bench. 1. The seat occupied by the judge in a courtroom <the judge called the lawyers to the bench for a sidebar>. **2.** The court considered in its official capacity <the judge's remarks from the bench influenced the jury>. **3.** Judges collectively <the federal bench attended a judicial-writing seminar>. **4.** The judges of a particular court <the Ninth Circuit bench>.

bench trial. A trial before a judge without a jury. ● In a bench trial, the judge decides questions of fact as well as questions of law.— Also termed *trial to the bench*; *nonjury trial*. Cf. JURY TRIAL.

bench warrant. A warrant issued directly by a judge to a law-enforcement officer, esp. for the arrest of a person who has been held in contempt or has been indicted.

beneficiary. A person who is designated to benefit from an appointment, disposition, or assignment (as in a will, insurance policy, etc.); one designated to receive something as a result of a legal arrangement or instrument. See THIRD-PARTY BENEFICIARY.

benefit-of-the-bargain rule. The principle that a defrauded purchaser may recover the difference between the real value and the fraudulently represented value of the property purchased.

bequest, *n.* **1.** The act of giving property (usu. personal property) by will. **2.** Property (usu. personal property other than money) disposed of in a will. Cf. DEVISE; LEGACY.

best-evidence rule. The evidentiary rule providing that for a party to prove the contents of a writing (or a recording or photograph), the original must be produced unless it is unavailable, in which case secondary evidence—such as copies, notes, or testimony—may be admitted.

beyond a reasonable doubt. See REASONABLE DOUBT.

bill, *n.* **1.** A formal written complaint, such as a court paper requesting some specific action for reasons alleged <bill of review>. **2.** A legislative proposal offered for debate before its enactment <the House bill would raise taxes>. **3.** A bill of exchange; a draft <the bank would not honor the unsigned bill>. **4.** A formal document or note; an instrument <bill of sale>.

bill of exchange. See DRAFT.

bill of lading. A document of title acknowledging the receipt of goods by a carrier or by the shipper's agent; a document that indicates the receipt of goods for shipment and that is issued by a person engaged in the business of transporting or forwarding goods.

bill of rights. (*usu. cap.*) A section or addendum, usu. in a constitution, defining the situations in which a politically organized society will permit free, spontaneous, and individual activity, and guaranteeing that government powers will not be used in certain ways; esp., the first ten amendments to the U.S. Constitution.

binder. An insurer's memorandum giving the insured temporary coverage while the application for an insurance policy is being processed.

blackletter law. One or more legal principles that are fundamental and well settled <it is

blackletter law that a party must have standing to sue>.

Bluebook. The citation guide—formerly titled *A Uniform System of Citation*—that is generally considered the authoritative reference for American legal citations. ● The *Bluebook* is compiled by the editors of the *Columbia Law Review*, the *Harvard Law Review*, the *University of Pennsylvania Law Review*, and *The Yale Law Journal*.

blue-sky law. A state statute regulating the issuance and sale of securities, the purpose being to protect citizens from fraudulent investment schemes.

boilerplate. 1. Ready-made or all-purpose language that will fit in a variety of documents. **2.** Fixed or standardized contractual language that, in the view of the party whose forms contain it, is rarely subject to modification.

bona fide (**boh**-nə-**fid**-ee *or* **boh**-nə-fid), *adj.* [Latin "in good faith"] **1.** Made in good faith; without fraud or deceit. **2.** Sincere; genuine. See GOOD FAITH.

bona fide purchaser. One who buys something for value without notice of another's claim to the item or of any defects in the seller's title; one who has in good faith paid valuable consideration for property without notice of prior adverse claims.—Abbr. BFP.

bond, *n.* **1.** A written promise to pay money or do some act if certain circumstances occur. **2.** A long-term, interest-bearing debt instrument that is issued by a corporation or governmental entity usu. to provide for a particular financial need; esp., such an instrument in which the debt is secured by a lien on the issuer's property. Cf. DEBENTURE.

book, *vb.* To record the name of (a person arrested) in a sequential list of police arrests, with details of the person's identity (usu. including photographs and fingerprints), particulars about the alleged offense, and the name of the arresting officer <the defendant was booked immediately after his arrest>.

boycott, *n.* A concerted refusal to do business with a party in order to express disapproval of that party's practices.

breach of contract. Violation of a contractual obligation, either by failing to perform one's own promise or by interfering with the other party's performance.

breaking and entering. See BURGLARY (2).

bribery. The corrupt payment, receipt, or solicitation of a private favor for official action. ● Though a misdemeanor at common law, bribery is now a felony in most states.

brief, *n.* A written statement setting out the legal contentions of a party in litigation, esp. on appeal; a document prepared by counsel as the basis for arguing a case, consisting of legal and factual arguments and the authorities in support of them.

broker, *n.* An agent who acts as an intermediary or negotiator, esp. between prospective buyers and sellers (as of securities or real estate), for a fee or commission.

burden of persuasion. A party's duty to convince the fact-finder to view the facts in a way that favors that party. ● In civil cases the plaintiff's burden is usu. "by a preponderance of the evidence," while in criminal cases the prosecution's burden is "beyond a reasonable doubt."

burden of production. A party's duty to introduce enough evidence to have a given issue considered by the fact-finder. ● If a party fails to meet its burden of production, the judge can dismiss the case in a peremptory ruling such as a directed verdict.

bu den of proof. A party's duty to prove a disputed assertion or charge. • The burden of proof includes both the *burden of persuasion* and the *burden of production*.

burglary. 1. The common-law offense of breaking and entering another's dwelling at night with the intent to commit a felony. **2.** The modern statutory offense of breaking and entering any building—not just a dwelling, and not only at night—with the intent to commit a felony.—Also termed (in sense 2) *breaking and entering*. Cf. ROBBERY.

business-judgment rule. The presumption that in making business decisions not involving direct self-interest or self-dealing, corporate directors act on an informed basis, in good faith, and in the honest belief that their actions are in the corporation's best interest. • The rule shields directors and officers from liability for unprofitable or harmful corporate transactions if the transactions were made in good faith, with due care, and within the directors' or officers' authority.

bylaw. A rule or administrative provision adopted by an association or corporation for its internal governance. • Corporate bylaws are usu. enacted apart from the articles of incorporation.

C

capacity. **1.** The role in which one performs an act <in his official capacity>. **2.** A legal qualification, such as legal age, that determines one's ability to sue or be sued, to enter into a binding contract, and the like <she had capacity to enter into the lease>. **3.** The mental ability to understand the nature and effects of one's acts <his severe pain reduced his capacity to understand the hospital's medical-consent form>. See COMPETENCY.

capital, *n.* **1.** Money or assets invested, or available for investment, in a business <they raised enough capital to start a new company>. **2.** The total amount or value of a corporation's stock; corporate equity <AT&T's stated capital>. **3.** The total assets of a business, esp. those that help generate profits; net worth <the manufacturer bought more equipment in an effort to increase its capital>.

caption. The introductory part of a court paper, stating the names of the parties, the name of the court, the docket or file number, and the title of the action.

care, *n.* In the law of negligence, the conduct demanded of a person in a given situation. ● Typically, this involves a person's giving attention both to possible dangers, mistakes, and pitfalls and to ways of ensuring that these risks do not materialize. See REASONABLE PERSON.

case. A proceeding, action, suit, or controversy at law or in equity <the parties settled the case>.

casebook. A law-school textbook containing the leading cases in a field, usu. with commentary on and questions about the cases. Cf. HORNBOOK.

case-in-chief. The part of a trial in which the party with the burden of proof presents evidence.

caselaw. The collection of reported cases that form the common law within a given jurisdiction. See COMMON LAW (1).

cause of action. 1. A group of operative facts, such as a harmful act, giving rise to one or more bases for suing <the surgeon's conduct gave rise to the family's cause of action>. **2.** A legal theory of a lawsuit <a fraud cause of action>. **3.** Loosely, a lawsuit <there are four defendants in the pending cause of action>.

caveat emptor (**kav**-ee-aht **em[p]**-tər *or*-tor). [Latin "let the buyer beware"] A doctrine

29

holding that purchasers buy at their own risk.
● Modern statutes and cases have greatly limited the importance of this doctrine.

cease-and-desist order. A court order or
agency order prohibiting a person from continuing a particular course of conduct. See IN-
JUNCTION; RESTRAINING ORDER.

certiorari (sər-sh[ee]ə-**rahr**-ee *or* -**rer**-ee *or*
-**rer**-I). [Latin "to be informed"] An extraordinary writ issued by an appellate court, at its
discretion, directing a lower court to deliver
the record in the case for review. ● Certiorari
is used by the U.S. Supreme Court to review
most of the cases it decides to hear.—Abbr.
cert.—Also termed *writ of certiorari*.

CFR. *abbr.* CODE OF FEDERAL REGULATIONS.

chain of custody. The movement and location of evidence from the time it is obtained to
the time it is presented in court <the detective
testified about the handgun's chain of custo-
dy>.

chain of title. 1. The ownership history of a
piece of land, from its first owner to the present one. **2.** The ownership history of a negotiable instrument, traceable through its indorse-
ments. ● For the holder to have good title,
every prior negotiation must have been proper.

If a necessary indorsement is missing or forged, the chain of title is broken and no later transferee can become a holder.

challenge, *n.* **1.** An act or instance of formally questioning the legality or legal qualifications of a person, action, or thing <a challenge to whether the witness had personal knowledge>. **2.** A party's request that a judge disqualify a potential juror or an entire jury panel <the defendant's attorney used a challenge on a panelist who had recently been mugged>.

chambers. A judge's private office. See IN CAMERA.

chancery. 1. A court of equity. **2.** The system of jurisprudence administered in courts of equity. See EQUITY.

change of venue. The removal of a case from one locale to another, usu. because of questions of fairness.—Also termed *transfer of venue.* See VENUE.

Chapter 7. 1. The chapter of the Bankruptcy Code calling for the collection and liquidation of a debtor's property, voluntarily or by court order, to satisfy creditors. **2.** A bankruptcy case filed under this chapter. See LIQUIDATION (4).

Chapter 11. 1. The chapter of the Bankruptcy Code allowing an insolvent business, or one that is threatened with insolvency, to reorganize itself under court supervision while continuing its normal operations and restructuring its debt. ● Although the Code does not expressly prohibit the use of Chapter 11 by an individual nonbusiness debtor, the vast majority of Chapter 11 cases involve business debtors. **2.** A bankruptcy case filed under this chapter. See REORGANIZATION.

Chapter 13. 1. The chapter of the Bankruptcy Code calling for a person's future earnings to be placed under the supervision of a trustee until all unsecured creditors are satisfied. **2.** A bankruptcy case filed under this chapter.

character witness. A witness who testifies about another person's character traits or community reputation.

charge, *n.* **1.** A formal accusation of a crime as a preliminary step in prosecution <a manslaughter charge>. **2.** JURY CHARGE <after closing arguments, the judge read the charge to the jury>.

charter, *n.* **1.** An instrument by which a governmental entity grants rights, liberties, or powers to its citizens. **2.** A legislative act that creates a business or defines a corporate franchise. Cf. ARTICLES OF INCORPORATION.

chattel (**chat**-[ə]l). (*usu. pl.*) Movable or transferable property; any property other than freehold land, esp. personal property.

check, *n.* A draft that is signed by the maker or drawer, drawn on a bank, payable on demand, and unlimited in negotiability. See DRAFT.

child support. 1. A parent's legal obligation to contribute to the economic maintenance and education of children. **2.** In a custody or divorce action, the money paid by one parent to the other for the expenses incurred for children of the marriage. Cf. ALIMONY.

choice of law. In conflict of laws, the question of which jurisdiction's law should apply in a given case. See CONFLICT OF LAWS.

circumstantial evidence. Evidence based on inference rather than on personal knowledge or observation.—Also termed *indirect evidence*. Cf. DIRECT EVIDENCE.

citation. 1. A court-issued writ that commands a person to appear at a certain time and place to do something demanded in the writ, or to show cause for not doing so <John-

son was served with a citation while at the office>. **2.** A reference to a legal precedent or authority (such as a case, statute, or treatise) to support a given position <the brief was full of citations to cases>.—Also termed (in sense 2) *cite.*

civil action. A judicial proceeding brought to enforce, redress, or protect a private or civil right; a noncriminal case.

civil law. 1. (*usu. cap.*) One of the two prominent legal systems in the Western World, originally administered in the Roman Empire and still in effect in continental Europe, Latin America, Scotland, and Louisiana, among other parts of the world. Cf. COMMON LAW (2). **2.** The body of law imposed by the state, as opposed to moral law. **3.** The law of civil or private rights, as opposed to criminal law or administrative law.

civil procedure. The body of law that governs the methods and practices used in civil litigation, such as the Federal Rules of Civil Procedure.

civil right. (*usu. pl.*) The individual rights of personal liberty guaranteed by the Bill of Rights and by the 13th, 14th, 15th, and 19th Amendments, as well as by legislation such as the Voting Rights Act. ● Civil rights include esp. the right to vote, the right of due process, and the right of equal protection under the law.

claim, *n.* **1.** The aggregate of operative facts giving rise to a right enforceable by a court <the plane crash led to dozens of wrongful-death claims>. **2.** The assertion of an existing right; any right to payment or to an equitable remedy, even if contingent or provisional <an employee's claim for workers'-compensation benefits>. **3.** A demand for money or property to which one asserts a right <the letter included a claim for attorney's fees>.

class action. A lawsuit in which a single person or a small group of people represent by their litigation the interests of a larger group. ● Federal procedure has several requirements for maintaining a class action: (1) the class must be so large that individual suits would be impracticable, (2) there must be legal or factual questions common to the class, (3) the claims or defenses of the representative parties must be typical of those of the class, and (4) the representative parties must adequately protect the interests of the class.

clean-hands doctrine. The principle that a party cannot take advantage of its own wrong by seeking equitable relief or asserting an equitable defense if that party has violated an equitable principle, such as good faith. ● Such a party is described as having "unclean hands."—Also termed *unclean-hands doctrine*.

clear and convincing evidence. Evidence indicating that the thing to be proved is highly probable or reasonably certain. ● This is a greater burden than preponderance of the evidence, the standard applied in most civil cases, but less than evidence beyond a reasonable doubt, the norm for criminal trials. Clear and convincing evidence is usu. the standard in cases involving the termination of parental rights.

clemency. Mercy or leniency; esp., the power of the President or a governor to pardon or commute a criminal sentence.

clerk. 1. A public official whose duties include keeping records or accounts. **2.** A court officer responsible for filing papers, issuing process, and keeping records of court proceedings as generally specified by rule or statute.—Also termed *clerk of court*. **3.** A law student or recent law-school graduate who assists a lawyer or judge with legal research, writing, and other tasks.—Also termed *law clerk*.

close corporation. A corporation whose stock is not freely traded and is held by only a few shareholders (often within the same family). ● The requirements and privileges of close corporations vary by jurisdiction.—Also termed *closely held corporation*; *closed corporation*.

closing. In the sale of real estate, the final transaction between the buyer and seller, during which the conveyancing documents are concluded and the money and property transferred.

closing argument. In a trial, a lawyer's final statement to the judge or jury before deliberation begins, in which the lawyer requests the judge or jury to consider the evidence and to apply the law in his or her client's favor.—Also termed *closing statement*; *summation*.

cloud on title. A defect or potential defect in the owner's title to a piece of land arising from some claim or encumbrance, such as a lien, an easement, or a court order.

code. A complete system of positive law, carefully arranged and officially promulgated; a systematic collection or revision of laws, rules, or regulations <the penal code>. ● Strictly, a code is a compilation not just of existing statutes, but also of much of the unwritten law on a subject, which is newly enacted as a complete system of law.

Code of Federal Regulations. The annual collection of executive-agency regulations published in the daily Federal Register, combined with previously issued regulations that are still in effect.—Abbr. CFR.

codicil (**kod**-ə-səl *or* -sil). A supplement or addition to a will, not necessarily disposing of the entire estate but modifying, explaining, or otherwise qualifying the will in some way. ● When admitted to probate, the codicil becomes a part of the will.

collateral, *n.* Property pledged by a borrower as security for the debt.

collateral attack. An attack on a judgment entered in an earlier proceeding. ● A petition for a writ of habeas corpus is one type of collateral attack. Cf. DIRECT ATTACK.

collateral estoppel. An affirmative defense barring a party from relitigating an issue determined against that party in an earlier action, even if the second action differs significantly from the earlier one. Cf. RES JUDICATA.

collective bargaining. Negotiations between an employer and the representatives of organized employees for the purpose of determining the conditions of employment, such as wages, hours, and fringe benefits.

collusion. An agreement between two or more persons to defraud another or to obtain something forbidden by law.

comity (**kom**-ə-tee). Courtesy among political entities (such as nations, states, or courts of different jurisdictions), involving esp. mutual recognition of legislative, executive, and judicial acts.

commercial law. The substantive law dealing with the sale and distribution of goods, the financing of credit transactions on the security of the goods sold, and negotiable instruments. • Most American commercial law is governed by the Uniform Commercial Code.

commercial paper. Negotiable instruments collectively, esp. in the form of drafts or notes.—Often shortened to *paper*.

commercial speech. Communication (such as advertising and marketing) that involves only the commercial interests of the speaker and the audience, and is therefore afforded lesser First Amendment protection than social, political, or religious speech.

commitment. The act of confining a person in a prison, mental hospital, or other institution <the court ordered a civil commitment of Burgess, who had been diagnosed as being schizophrenic>.

common law. 1. The body of law derived from judicial decisions and opinions, rather than from statutes or constitutions. See CASE-LAW. **2.** The body of law based on the English legal system, as distinct from a civil-law system. ● All states except Louisiana have the common law as their legal system. Cf. CIVIL LAW (1).

common-law marriage. A marriage that takes legal effect, without license or ceremony, when a couple live together as husband and wife, intend to be married, and hold themselves out to others as a married couple. ● Common-law marriages are permitted in 15 states and in the District of Columbia.

common stock. Stock that gives its holders the right to vote and to receive dividends after other claims and dividends have been paid (esp. to preferred shareholders). Cf. PREFERRED STOCK.

community property. In some states, property owned in common by husband and wife as a result of its having been acquired during the marriage by means other than gift or inheritance, each spouse holding a one-half interest in the property. ● Only nine states have community-property systems: Arizona, California, Idaho, Louisiana, Nevada, New Mexico, Texas, Washington, and Wisconsin. Cf. SEPARATE PROPERTY.

comparative negligence. A plaintiff's own negligence that proportionally reduces the damages recoverable from a defendant. Cf. CONTRIBUTORY NEGLIGENCE.

compensatory damages. See ACTUAL DAMAGES.

competence. 1. A basic or minimal ability to do something; qualification, esp. to testify <competence of an expert witness>. 2. The capacity of an official body to do something <the court's competence to enter a valid judgment>. 3. Admissibility <competence of the evidence>.

competency. The mental ability to understand problems and make decisions. ● In the context of a criminal defendant's ability to stand trial, competency includes the capacity

41

to understand the proceedings, to consult meaningfully with counsel, and to assist in the defense.

complaint. 1. The initial pleading that starts a civil action and states the grounds for the court's jurisdiction, the plaintiff's claim, and the demand for relief. ● In some states, this pleading is called a *petition*. Cf. ANSWER. **2.** In criminal law, a formal charge accusing a person of an offense. Cf. INDICTMENT; INFORMATION.

conclusion of law. A judicial deduction made on a showing of certain facts, no further evidence being required; a legal inference mandated by the evidence. Cf. FINDING OF FACT.

conclusive presumption. A presumption that cannot be overcome by any additional evidence or argument <it is a conclusive presumption that a child under the age of seven is incapable of committing a felony>.—Also termed *irrebuttable presumption*. Cf. REBUTTABLE PRESUMPTION.

concurrence. 1. A vote cast by a judge in favor of the judgment reached, often on grounds differing from those expressed in the majority opinion explaining the judgment. **2.** A separate written opinion explaining such a vote.—Also termed (in sense 2) *concurring opinion*.

concurrent sentences. Two or more overlapping periods of jail time to be served simultaneously. ● For example, if a defendant receives concurrent sentences of 5 years and 15 years, the total amount of jail time is 15 years. Cf. CONSECUTIVE SENTENCES.

condemnation. The determination and declaration that certain property (esp. land) is taken for public use, subject to reasonable compensation; the exercise of eminent domain by a governmental entity. See EMINENT DOMAIN.

condition. 1. A stipulation or prerequisite in a contract, will, or other instrument. **2.** A future and uncertain event on which the existence or extent of an obligation or liability depends; an uncertain act or event that triggers or negates a duty to render a promised performance. ● For example, if Smith promises to pay Jones $500 for repairing a car, Jones's failure to repair the car (a condition) relieves Smith of the promise to pay. **3.** A qualification attached to the conveyance of property providing that if a particular event does or does not take place, the estate will be created, enlarged, defeated, or transferred.

condition precedent. An act or event, other than a lapse of time, that must exist or occur before a duty to perform a promised performance arises. ● If the condition does not occur and is not excused, the promised performance need not be rendered. The most common condition contemplated by this term is the immediate or unconditional duty of performance by a promisor.

condition subsequent. A condition that, if it occurs, will bring something else to an end; an event the existence of which, by agreement of the parties, operates to discharge a duty of performance that has arisen.

confession. A criminal suspect's admission of guilt, usu. in writing and often including a disclosure of details about the crime.

conflict of interest. 1. A real or apparent incompatibility between one's private interests and one's public or fiduciary duties. **2.** A real or apparent incompatibility between the interests of two of a lawyer's clients, such that the lawyer is disqualified from representing both clients if the dual representation adversely affects either client or if the clients do not consent.

conflict of laws. 1. A difference between the laws of different states or countries in a case in which a party has acquired rights within two or more jurisdictions. **2.** The body of jurisprudence that undertakes to reconcile such differences or to decide what law is to govern in those situations; the principles of choice of law.

Confrontation Clause. The Sixth Amendment provision guaranteeing a criminal defendant's right to cross-examine any witness.

consecutive sentences. Two or more periods of jail time to be served in sequence. ● For example, if a defendant receives consecutive sentences of 20 years and 5 years, the total amount of the jail time is 25 years.—Also termed *cumulative sentences*. Cf. CONCURRENT SENTENCES.

conservator. A person appointed by the court to manage the estate or affairs of someone who is legally incapable of doing so.

consideration. Something of value (such as an act, a forbearance, or a return promise) received by one party to a contract from the other party. ● Consideration, or a substitute such as promissory estoppel, is necessary for a contract to be enforceable.

consignment. 1. The transfer of goods to the custody of another (the *consignee*) for future delivery or sale. **2.** The goods so transferred. ● When a merchant takes goods on consignment, the usual agreement is that the owner (the *consignor*) will be paid only for goods that are sold, and that any unsold goods will be returned to the owner.

conspiracy. An agreement by two or more persons to commit an unlawful act; a combination for an unlawful purpose. ● In criminal law, conspiracy is a separate offense from the crime that is the object of the conspiracy.

constitution. 1. The fundamental law of a nation or state, establishing the conception, character, and organization of its government, as well as prescribing the extent of its sovereign power and the manner in which this power is exercised. **2.** The written instrument embodying this fundamental law.

constitutional law. The body of law deriving from the U.S. Constitution (or a state constitution) and dealing primarily with governmental powers and civil rights and liberties.

constitutional tort. A violation of one's constitutional rights by a government officer, redressable by a civil action filed directly against the officer. ● Constitutional torts committed under color of state law (such as civil-rights violations) can be redressed in federal court.

construction. The act or process of interpreting or explaining the sense or intention of a writing (usu. a statute, opinion, or instrument).

constructive, *adj.* Legally imputed; having an effect in law though not necessarily in fact <constructive knowledge> <constructive fraud>. ● Courts usu. give something a constructive effect for equitable reasons.

constructive notice. Notice arising by presumption of law from the existence of facts and circumstances that a party had a duty to take notice of, such as a registered deed or a pending lawsuit; notice presumed by law to have been acquired by a person and thus imputed to that person. Cf. ACTUAL NOTICE.

constructive trust. A trust imposed by a court on equitable grounds against one who has obtained property by wrongdoing, thus preventing the wrongful holder from being unjustly enriched. ● A constructive trust does not create a fiduciary relationship. Cf. RESULT-ING TRUST.

contempt. Conduct that defies the authority or dignity of a court or legislature. ● Because contempt interferes with the administration of justice, it is punishable, usu. by fine or imprisonment.

contingent fee. A fee charged for a lawyer's services only if the lawsuit is successful or is favorably settled out of court. ● Contingent fees are usu. calculated as a percentage of the client's recovery, such as 33% of the recovery if the case is settled, and 40% if the case is won at trial.—Also termed *contingency fee*.

continuance. The adjournment or postponement of a trial or other proceeding until a future date <the court granted a continuance because discovery wasn't complete>.

contract, *n.* **1.** An agreement between two or more parties creating obligations that are enforceable or otherwise recognizable at law <a contract for the sale of a house>. **2.** The writing that sets forth such an agreement <Follett misplaced the signed contract>. **3.** The body of law dealing with agreements and exchange <the plaintiff sued in contract and in tort>.

contribution. The right that gives one of several persons who are liable on a common debt the ability to recover from each of the others in proportion when that one person discharges the debt for the benefit of all; the right to demand that another who is jointly responsible for a third party's injury pay part of what one is required to compensate the third party. Cf. INDEMNITY.

contributory negligence. A plaintiff's own negligence that played a part in causing the plaintiff's injury and that is significant enough to bar the plaintiff from recovering damages. ● In most states, this defense has been superseded by comparative negligence. Cf. COMPARATIVE NEGLIGENCE.

conversion. In tort and criminal law, the wrongful possession or disposition of another's personal property as if it were one's own.

conveyance. 1. The voluntary transfer of a right. **2.** The transfer of an interest in real property from one living person to another, by means of an instrument such as a deed. **3.** The document (usu. a deed) by which such a transfer occurs.

conviction, *n.* **1.** The act or process of judicially finding someone guilty of a crime; the state of having been proved guilty. **2.** The judgment (as by a jury verdict) that a person is guilty of a crime.

copyright. A property right in an original work of authorship fixed in any tangible medium of expression (such as a literary, musical, artistic, photographic, or film work), giving the holder the exclusive right to reproduce, adapt, distribute, perform, and display the work. • Federal copyright law is governed by the Copyright Act of 1976.

corporation. A statutory entity (usu. a business) having authority to act as a legal person distinct from the shareholders who make it up and having rights to issue stock and to exist indefinitely.

corporeal (kor-**por**-ee-əl), *adj*. Having a physical material existence; tangible <land and fixtures are corporeal property>. Cf. INCORPO-REAL.

corpus (**kor**-pəs). [Latin "body"] **1.** The property for which a trustee is responsible; the trust principal.—Also termed *res*; *trust estate*. **2.** Principal (as of a fund or estate), as opposed to interest or income. Pl. **corpora.**

corroboration. (kə-rob-ə-**ray**-shən). Confirmation or support by additional evidence or authority <the bystanders provided corroboration of the plaintiff's testimony>.

counsel, *n.* **1.** Advice or assistance <the defendant refused to follow her lawyer's counsel to accept the plea bargain>. **2.** One or more lawyers who represent a client <the corporation had several attorneys as counsel of record in the case>.—In the singular, also termed *counselor.*

count, *n.* **1.** The part of an indictment charging the suspect with a distinct offense. **2.** In pleading, the plaintiff's statement of a distinct claim.

counterclaim. A defendant's claim in opposition to, or as a setoff against, the plaintiff's claim <in response to the creditor's lawsuit, Lang filed a counterclaim for fraud>. Cf. CROSS-CLAIM.

counteroffer. In contract law, an offeree's new offer that varies the terms of the original offer. • By varying the terms, the offeree rejects the original offer.

course of dealing. An established pattern of conduct between the parties to a business transaction. • If a dispute arises, the parties' course of dealing can be used as evidence of how they intended to carry out the transaction.

court. **1.** A governmental body consisting of one or more judges who sit to adjudicate disputes and administer justice <the couple had to go to court to adopt the infant>. **2.** The judge or judges who sit on such a governmental body <the court declared a mistrial>.

court costs. The charges or fees assessed by a court, such as filing fees, jury fees, reporter fees, and courthouse fees.

court order. See ORDER (1).

court reporter. A person who transcribes by shorthand, stenographically takes down, or electronically records testimony during court proceedings or trial-related proceedings.

court rules. Regulations having the force of law and governing practice and procedure in the various courts, such as the Federal Rules of Civil and Criminal Procedure, the U.S. Supreme Court Rules, and the Federal Rules of Evidence, as well as any local rules that a particular court promulgates.

covenant, *n.* **1.** A formal agreement or promise, usu. in a contract. **2.** A promise made in a deed or implied by law; esp., an obligation in a deed burdening or favoring a landowner.

covenant not to compete. See NONCOMPETI-
TION CLAUSE.

creditor. One to whom a debt (esp. money) is
owed.

crime. A social harm that the law makes
punishable; the breach of a legal duty treated
as the subject matter of criminal proceedings.

criminal action. A judicial proceeding instituted by the government to punish offenses
against the public; a prosecution.

criminal law. The body of law defining offenses against the community at large, regulating how suspects are investigated, charged,
and tried, and establishing punishments for
convicted offenders.

criminal procedure. The legal rules governing the methods by which crimes are investigated, prosecuted, adjudicated, and punished,
as well as the protection of accused persons'
constitutional rights.

cross-claim. A claim that arises between co-
defendants or coplaintiffs in a case and that
relates to the subject of the original claim or
counterclaim <the defendants in the asbestos
suit filed cross-claims against each other>.—
Also termed *cross-action*. Cf. COUNTERCLAIM.

cross-examination. The formal questioning of a witness by the opponent of the party who called the witness to testify. ● The cross-examiner is typically allowed to ask leading questions but is usu. limited to matters covered on direct examination and to credibility issues.— Often shortened to *cross*. Cf. DIRECT EXAMINATION.

cumulative sentences. See CONSECUTIVE SENTENCES.

custody. 1. The care and control of a thing or person for inspection, preservation, or security. **2.** The care, control, and maintenance of a child awarded by a court to one of the parents in a divorce or separation proceeding.

D

D.A. *abbr*. DISTRICT ATTORNEY.

damages. Money claimed by, or ordered to be paid to, a person as compensation for loss or injury caused by a wrongdoer <the plaintiff seeks $8,000 in damages from the defendant>.

deadly force. Violent action known to create a substantial risk of causing death or serious bodily harm. ● In most states, a person may use deadly force in self-defense only if retaliating against another's deadly force.

dead man's statute. A law prohibiting the admission of a decedent's statements as evidence in certain circumstances, as when an opposing party or witness seeks to use those statements to support a claim against the decedent's estate.—Also termed *dead person's statute*.

debenture. **1.** A debt secured only by the debtor's earning power, not by any specific asset; an instrument acknowledging such a debt. **2.** A bond that is backed only by the general credit and financial reputation of the corporate issuer, not by a lien on corporate assets. Cf. BOND (2).

debt. 1. Liability on a claim; a specific sum of money due by agreement or otherwise <the debt amounted to $2,500>. **2.** The aggregate of all existing claims against a person, entity, or state <because he had accumulated so much debt, Ted filed for bankruptcy>.

debtor. 1. One who owes an obligation to another, esp. an obligation to pay money. **2.** A person or entity that is the subject of a bankruptcy case. ● The Bankruptcy Code refers to the "debtor" rather than the "bankrupt."

decedent (də-**seed**-[ə]nt), *n*. A dead person, esp. one who has died recently.

decision. A judicial determination after consideration of the facts and the law; esp., a ruling, order, or judgment pronounced by a court when considering or disposing of a case.

declaration. 1. A formal statement, proclamation, or announcement, esp. one embodied in an instrument. **2.** A document that governs legal rights to certain types of real property, such as a condominium or a residential subdivision. **3.** An unsworn statement made by someone having knowledge of facts relating to an event in dispute.

declaratory judgment. A binding adjudication that establishes the rights and other legal relations of the parties without providing for or ordering enforcement. ● Declaratory judgments are often sought by insurance companies to determine whether a policy covers a given party or claim.

decree, *n.* A court order, esp. one in a domestic-relations case <divorce decree>.

deed. A written instrument by which land is conveyed.

deed of trust. A deed conveying title to real property to a trustee as security until the grantor repays a loan. ● This type of deed resembles a mortgage.

de facto (də-**fak**-toh *or* day-), *adj.* Existing in fact; actual; having effect even though not formally or legally recognized <de facto segregation>. Cf. DE JURE.

defamation. 1. The act of harming the reputation of another by making a false statement to a third person. **2.** A false written or oral statement that damages another's reputation. See LIBEL; SLANDER.

default judgment. 1. A judgment entered against a defendant who has failed to answer, appear at trial, or otherwise defend against the plaintiff's claim. **2.** A judgment entered as a penalty against a party who has not complied with an order, esp. an order to provide or permit discovery.

defect, *n.* An imperfection or shortcoming, esp. in a part that is essential to the operation or safety of a product <the expert testified that the airbag had a manufacturing defect>. See PRODUCTS LIABILITY.

defendant. A person sued in a civil proceeding or accused in a criminal proceeding. Cf. PLAINTIFF.

defense. 1. A defendant's statement of a reason why the plaintiff or prosecutor has no valid case against the defendant; esp., a defendant's answer, denial, or plea <her defense was that she was 25 miles from the building at the time of the burglary>. **2.** A defendant's method and strategy in opposing the plaintiff or the prosecution <the lawyer advised his client that the best defense was to plead guilty and hope for probation>.

deficiency, *n.* **1.** A shortfall in paying taxes; the amount by which the tax properly due exceeds the sum of the amount of tax shown on a taxpayer's return plus amounts previously assessed or collected as a deficiency, minus any credits, refunds, or other payments due the taxpayer. **2.** The amount still owed on a secured debt (such as a mortgage) after the sale of the secured property fails to yield sufficient proceeds to cover the debt's full amount; esp., the shortfall between the proceeds of a foreclosure sale and the principal debt plus interest together with the foreclosure costs.

degree. An incremental measure of guilt or negligence; a grade based on the seriousness of an offense <murder in the second degree>.

de jure (də-**juur**-ee *or* day-**juur**-ay), *adj.* Existing by right or according to law <de jure segregation>. Cf. DE FACTO.

delivery. The formal act of transferring or conveying something, such as a deed; the thing so transferred or conveyed.

demand, *n.* **1.** The assertion of a legal right. **2.** A request for payment of a debt or an amount due.

demise, *n.* **1.** The conveyance of an estate by will or lease; the instrument by which such a conveyance is accomplished <the demise of the farm for 20 years>. **2.** The passing of property by descent or by will <Clara's demise of $20,000 to the hospital>.

demonstrative evidence. Physical evidence that one can see and inspect, such as a model or photograph.

denial. 1. A refusal or rejection <denial of the employment application>; esp., a court's refusal to grant a request presented in a motion or petition <the denial of the motion surprised the defense>. **2.** A defendant's response contradicting the facts that a plaintiff has alleged in a complaint; a repudiation <the defendant filed a sworn denial>.

deponent. A witness who testifies by deposition.

deposition (de-pə-**zi**-shən). **1.** A witness's out-of-court testimony that is reduced to writing (usu. by a court reporter) for later use in court or for discovery purposes. **2.** The session at which such testimony is recorded.

derivative action. A suit by a beneficiary of a fiduciary to enforce a right belonging to the fiduciary; esp., a suit asserted by a shareholder on the corporation's behalf against a third party (usu. a corporate officer) because of the corporation's failure to take some action against the third party.—Also termed *shareholder derivative suit*.

60

descent. The acquisition of real property by act of law, as by inheritance; the passing of intestate real property to heirs. Cf. DISTRIBUTION.

detrimental reliance. Reliance by one party on the acts or representations of another, resulting in a worsening of the first party's position. ● Detrimental reliance may serve as a substitute for consideration and thus make a promise enforceable as a contract. See PROMISSORY ESTOPPEL.

devise, *n.* **1.** The act of giving property (usu. real property) by will; the provision in a will containing such a gift. **2.** Property (usu. real property) disposed of in a will. Cf. BEQUEST; LEGACY.

dictum. A judicial comment made during the course of delivering a judicial opinion, but one that is unnecessary to the decision in the case and therefore not precedential (though it may be considered persuasive).—Also termed *obiter dictum*. Pl. **dicta.** Cf. HOLDING (1).

digest, *n.* An index of reported cases arranged by subject and subdivided by jurisdiction and court, providing brief statements of the facts and the court holdings.

direct attack. An attack on a judgment made in the same proceeding as the one in which the judgment was entered. • Examples of direct attacks are appeals and motions for new trial. Cf. COLLATERAL ATTACK.

directed verdict. A judgment entered on the order of a trial judge who takes over the fact-finding role of the jury because the evidence is so compelling that only one decision can reasonably follow or because the evidence fails to establish a prima facie case.—Also termed *instructed verdict*.

direct evidence. Evidence that is based on personal knowledge or observation and that, if true, proves a fact without inference or presumption. Cf. CIRCUMSTANTIAL EVIDENCE.

direct examination. The first questioning of a witness in a trial or other proceeding, conducted by the party who called the witness to testify.—Often shortened to *direct*. Cf. CROSS-EXAMINATION.

disability. Lack of a legal qualification; incapacity <a minor's disabilities>.

discharge, *vb*. **1.** To pay or satisfy (a debt or some other obligation) <Tubb had to discharge all her debts before applying for the loan>. **2.** To release (a debtor) from monetary obligations upon adjudication of bankruptcy <in his Chapter 7 bankruptcy, Smith was discharged from his debts>.

disciplinary rule. A mandatory regulation stating the minimum level of professional conduct that a lawyer must sustain to avoid being subject to disciplinary action. ● These rules are found chiefly in the Model Code of Professional Responsibility.

disclaimer. 1. A renunciation or denial of one's own or another's legal right or claim. **2.** A writing that contains such a renunciation or denial.

discovery. The procedures, usu. conducted before trial, by which the parties to a case obtain relevant factual information from each other <the plaintiff was sanctioned for not responding to discovery>. ● The primary discovery devices are depositions, interrogatories, requests for admissions, and requests for production.

discretion. A public official's power or right to act in certain circumstances according to personal judgment and conscience. See ABUSE OF DISCRETION.

discretionary review. The form of appellate review that is not a matter of right but that occurs only when the higher court agrees to hear the case. See CERTIORARI.

discrimination. 1. The effect of a statute or established practice that confers privileges on a certain class or that denies privileges to another class because of race, age, sex, nationality, religion, or handicap. **2.** Differential treatment; esp., a failure to treat all persons equally when no reasonable distinction can be found between those favored and those not favored.

dishonor, *n.* The refusal to pay or accept a negotiable instrument (such as a check) when it is presented.

dismissal. Termination of an action or claim without further hearing, esp. before trial of the issues involved.

disposition. 1. The act of transferring something to another's care or possession, esp. by deed or will; the relinquishing of property <the disposition of Julia's estate>. **2.** A final settlement or determination <the court's disposition of the case without trial>.

dissent, *n.* **1.** A judge's disagreement with the decision reached by the majority. **2.** A separate written opinion explaining the judge's disagreement.—Also termed (in sense 2) *dissenting opinion*.

distribution. The passing of intestate personal property to heirs. Cf. DESCENT.

district attorney. A state official appointed or elected to represent the state in criminal cases in a particular judicial district; a prosecutor.—Abbr. D.A.

diversity jurisdiction. A federal court's exercise of authority over a case involving parties from different states and an amount in controversy greater than a statutory minimum (now $75,000). Cf. FEDERAL-QUESTION JURISDICTION.

dividend. A portion of a company's earnings or profits distributed proportionally to its shareholders.

divorce. The legal dissolution of a marriage by a court.—Also termed *marital dissolution*.

docket, *n.* **1.** A formal record in which a judge or court clerk briefly notes all the proceedings and filings in a court case <the clerk noted on the docket that the case had been settled>. **2.** A schedule of pending cases <the court had six cases set for trial on its Monday docket>.

doctor-patient privilege. The statutory right to exclude from evidence in a legal proceeding any communication a patient makes to a physician unless the patient consents to the disclosure.

document of title. A written description, identification, or declaration of goods authorizing the holder (usu. a bailee) to receive, hold, and dispose of the document and the goods it covers. ● Documents of title, such as bills of lading, warehouse receipts, and delivery orders, are governed by Article 7 of the UCC. See BAILMENT.

domestic relations. See FAMILY LAW.

domicile (**dom**-ə-sɪl *or* -səl *or* **doh**-mi-). **1.** The place where a person is physically present and that the person regards as home; a person's true, fixed, and permanent home and principal establishment, to which that person intends to return and remain even though he or she may for a time reside elsewhere. **2.** The residence of a person or corporation for legal purposes.

donor. 1. One who gives or confers something. **2.** The settlor of a trust.

double jeopardy. The fact of being prosecuted or punished twice for substantially the same offense. ● Double jeopardy is prohibited by the Fifth Amendment.

draft, *n.* An unconditional written order signed by one person (the *drawer*) directing another person (the *drawee* or *payor*) to pay a certain sum of money on demand or at a definite time to a named third person (the *payee*) or to bearer. ● A check is the most common example of a draft.—Also termed *bill of exchange*. Cf. NOTE.

dram-shop liability. Civil liability of a commercial seller of alcoholic beverages for personal injury caused by an intoxicated customer.

drawee. The person or entity that a draft is directed to and that is requested to pay the amount stated on it. ● The drawee is usu. a bank that is directed to pay a sum of money on a check or other instrument.—Also termed *payor*.

drawer. One who directs a person or entity, usu. a bank, to pay a sum of money stated in an instrument—for example, a person who writes a check; the maker of a note or draft.

due process. The conduct of legal proceedings according to the rules and principles established to protect and enforce private rights, including notice and the right to a fair hearing before a tribunal having the power to decide the case.

Due Process Clause. The constitutional provision that prohibits the government from unfairly or arbitrarily depriving a person of life, liberty, or property. • There are two Due Process Clauses in the U.S. Constitution, one in the Fifth Amendment applying to the federal government, and one in the Fourteenth Amendment applying to the states. Cf. EQUAL PROTECTION CLAUSE.

duress. Compulsion (esp. the threat of physical harm) illegally exercised to force a person to do something against his or her will. • A person who signs a contract under duress can usu. invalidate the contract. Also, a person can plead duress as a defense to an otherwise criminal act.

duty. 1. A legal obligation imposed by law or assumed voluntarily, for which somebody else has a corresponding right. **2.** Any action, performance, task, or observance required by a person in an official or fiduciary capacity. **3.** In tort law, a legal relationship arising from a standard of care, the violation of which subjects the actor to liability.

E

earnest money. A deposit paid by a buyer (esp. of real estate) both to hold a seller to a deal and to show good faith, and ordinarily forfeited if the buyer defaults.

easement. A legal or equitable right acquired by the owner of one piece of land (the *dominant estate*) to use another's land (the *servient estate*) for a special purpose, such as to drive through it to reach a highway. ● Unlike a lease or license, an easement lasts forever, but it does not give the owner a right to sell or improve the land.

ejectment. **1.** The ejection of an owner or occupier from property. **2.** A legal action by which a person wrongfully ejected from property seeks to recover possession and damages.

embezzlement. The fraudulent taking of personal property with which one has been entrusted, esp. as a fiduciary. ● The criminal intent for embezzlement—unlike larceny and false pretenses—arises after taking possession (not before or during the taking).

eminent domain. The power of a governmental entity to convert privately owned property, esp. land, to public use, subject to reasonable

compensation for the taking. See CONDEMNA-
TION.

emotional distress. Pain or suffering affecting the mind, often (but not necessarily) as a
result of physical injury.—Also termed *mental
anguish*. See INTENTIONAL INFLICTION OF EMOTION-
AL DISTRESS.

employee. One who works for another under
an express or implied contract. Cf. AGENT; INDE-
PENDENT CONTRACTOR.

en banc (on-**bonk** *or* en-**bank**). [French "on
the bench"] **1.** *adj.* Of or relating to a session
in which the full membership of the court
participates <an en banc proceeding>. **2.** *adv.*
With full membership; as a complete body
<the appellate court voted to hear the case en
banc>.

encumbrance. A claim or liability that is
attached to property or some other interest
and that may lessen its value, such as a lien or
mortgage. ● An encumbrance cannot defeat
the transfer of possession, but it remains after
the property or interest is transferred.—Also
spelled *incumbrance*.

enjoin, *vb.* To legally prohibit or restrain by
injunction <the court enjoined Barnes from
selling his new software>. See INJUNCTION.

entrapment. A law-enforcement officer's inducement of a person to commit a crime, for the purpose of bringing a criminal prosecution against that person.

equal protection. A constitutional requirement guaranteeing that similarly situated persons will receive the same legal rights.—Also termed *equal protection of the laws*.

Equal Protection Clause. The Fourteenth Amendment provision requiring that persons under like circumstances be given the same legal rights. Cf. DUE PROCESS CLAUSE.

equitable title. Title that indicates a beneficial interest in property and that gives the holder the right to receive formal legal title. Cf. LEGAL TITLE.

equity. 1. Fairness; impartiality; evenhanded dealing <Martin wanted his partners to treat him with equity>. **2.** The body of principles constituting what is fair and right; natural law <the court's decision seemed to be based on equity rather than on the evidence>. **3.** The recourse to principles of justice to correct or supplement the law as applied to particular circumstances <the court gave the plaintiff relief in equity because the injury was irreparable>. **4.** The amount by which the value of a property or an interest in property exceeds secured claims or liens <Paul had built up considerable equity in his home>. **5.** An ownership interest in property, esp. of shareholders in a business <all the senior employees were given equity in the company>.

***Erie* doctrine.** The principle that a federal court exercising diversity jurisdiction over a case that does not involve a federal question must apply the law of the state where the court sits. *Erie v. Tompkins*, 304 U.S. 64 (1938).

error. A mistake of law or of fact in a lower court's proceedings <the appellate court reversed the trial court's judgment because of numerous errors in the jury instructions>.

escheat, *n*. Reversion of property (esp. real property) to the state upon the death of an owner who has neither a will nor any legal heirs.

escrow, *n*. **1.** A legal document or property delivered by a promisor to a third party to be held by the third party for a given amount of time or until the occurrence of a condition, at which time the third party is to hand over the document or property to the promisee <the real-estate agent received the escrow shortly

before the closing date>. **2.** An account held in trust or as security <the earnest money is in escrow>.—Also termed *escrow account*. **3.** The holder of such a document, property, or account <the title company's representative acted as escrow>.—Also termed (in sense 3) *escrow agent*.

Establishment Clause. The constitutional provision (U.S. Const. amend. I) prohibiting the government from creating a church or favoring a particular religion. Cf. FREE EXERCISE CLAUSE.

estate. 1. All of a person's property considered as a whole <the decedent's taxable estate>. **2.** The amount, degree, or nature of a person's interest in property, esp. in land <a life estate>.

estate tax. A tax imposed on the estate of a decedent who transfers property by will or by intestate succession. ● The federal government imposes an estate tax on estates that are valued over a specified amount. Cf. INHERITANCE TAX.

estoppel (e-**stop**-əl). **1.** A legally imposed bar resulting from one's own conduct and precluding any denial or assertion regarding a fact. **2.** A doctrine that prevents a person from adopt-

73

ing an inconsistent position, attitude, or action if it will result in injury to another. **3.** An affirmative defense alleging good-faith reliance on a representation and an injury or detrimental change in position resulting from that reliance. Cf. WAIVER (1).

eviction. The act or process of legally dispossessing a person of land or rental property.

evidence, *n.* **1.** A perceptible thing that tends to establish the truth or falsity of an alleged fact, including testimony, documents, and other tangible objects <the prosecution's best evidence was the testimony of two eyewitnesses>. **2.** The collective mass of things, esp. testimony and exhibits, that are presented to a court in a given case <the jury discussed the evidence before voting>.

exclusionary rule. The rule providing that illegally obtained evidence is not admissible in court, often with the exception that the evidence is admissible when it was taken in the good-faith belief that it was legally obtained.

excuse, *n.* **1.** A reason that justifies an act or omission or relieves one of a duty. **2.** In criminal law, a defense that arises because the defendant is not blameworthy for having acted

in a way that would otherwise be criminal. ●
The following defenses are the traditional ex-
cuses: duress, entrapment, infancy, insanity,
and involuntary intoxication. Cf. JUSTIFICATION.

execution. 1. The act of carrying out or putting into effect (as an action or an order)
<execution of the court's decree>. **2.** Vali-
dation of a written instrument, such as a contract or will, by fulfilling the necessary legal
requirements <delivery of the goods completed the contract's execution>. **3.** Judicial enforcement of a money judgment, usu. by seiz-
ing and selling the judgment debtor's property
<the debtor's house was exempt from execu-
tion>. **4.** In criminal law, the carrying out of a
death sentence <the Supreme Court stayed
the execution>.

executor (ig-**zek**-yə-tər), *n.* One who is appointed by a testator, usu. in the will, to
administer the testator's estate. Cf. ADMINISTRA-
TOR.

executory interest. A future interest, held
by a third person, that either cuts off another's interest or begins after the natural termination of a preceding estate.

exemplary damages. See PUNITIVE DAMAGES.

exempt property. 1. A debtor's holdings and possessions that, by law, a creditor cannot seize to satisfy a debt. ● The property that creditors may lawfully reach is known as *nonexempt property*. **2.** Personal property that a surviving spouse is automatically entitled to receive from the decedent's estate.

exhaustion of remedies. The doctrine that, if an administrative remedy is provided by statute, a claimant must seek relief first from the administrative body before judicial relief is available.

exhibit, *n.* **1.** A document, record, or other tangible object formally introduced as evidence in court <the defendant didn't offer any exhibits>. **2.** A document attached to and made part of a pleading, motion, contract, or other instrument <the promissory note was attached to the complaint as Exhibit A>.

ex parte (eks-**pahr**-tee *or* -tay). [Latin "from the part"] **1.** *adv.* On or from one party only, usu. without notice to or argument from the adverse party <the lawyer's phone call to the judge was made ex parte>. **2.** *adj.* Done or made at the instance and for the benefit of one party only, and without notice to, or argument by, any person adversely interested <an ex parte temporary restraining order>.

expert witness. A witness qualified by knowledge, skill, experience, training, or education to provide scientific, technical, or other specialized opinions about the evidence or a fact issue <the prosecution's expert witness testified about the DNA evidence>.—Often shortened to *expert*. Cf. LAY WITNESS.

ex post facto law. A law passed after an action in order to retroactively change the legal treatment of the action to the disadvantage of the actor. • Ex post facto criminal laws are prohibited by Article I of the U.S. Constitution.

express, *adj.* Clearly and unmistakably communicated; directly stated rather than implied <express authority> <an express condition>. Cf. IMPLIED.

express trust. A trust created with the settlor's express intent, usu. declared in writing; an ordinary trust as opposed to a resulting trust or a constructive trust.

express warranty. A warranty created by the overt words or actions of the seller. Cf. IMPLIED WARRANTY.

expungement of record. The removal of a conviction (esp. for a first offense) from a person's criminal record. • Expungement does not occur automatically, but some states allow criminal records to be expunged and sealed if the applicant requests it in writing and is facing no new charges.

extortion. The act or practice of obtaining something (esp. money) or compelling some action by illegal means, such as force or coercion.

extradition. The surrender of an alleged criminal by one state or nation to another having jurisdiction over the crime charged <the United States sought extradition of the suspected terrorists from France>.

extraordinary writ. A writ issued by a court exercising unusual or discretionary power. ● Examples of extraordinary writs are certiorari, habeas corpus, mandamus, and prohibition.

eyewitness. One who personally observes an event.

F

fact-finder. One or more persons—such as jurors in a jury trial or administrative-law judges in a hearing—who hear testimony and review evidence to make the ultimate ruling about a factual issue such as whether certain events took place.—Also termed *finder of fact*. See FINDING OF FACT.

false imprisonment. A confinement or restraint of a person to a bounded area without justification or consent <the plaintiff, who had not shoplifted, sued the department store for false imprisonment because the security guards kept him for three hours>. ● False imprisonment is both a common-law misdemeanor and a tort.

false pretenses. The crime of knowingly obtaining title to another's personal property by means of misrepresenting a fact with the intent to defraud.

family court. A court having jurisdiction over matters involving divorce, child custody and support, paternity, domestic violence, and other family-law issues.

family law. The body of law dealing with marriage, divorce, adoption, child custody and support, and other domestic-relations issues.—

Also termed *domestic relations*; *domestic-relations law*.

federal common law. The body of decisional law developed by federal courts adjudicating federal questions and other matters of federal concern, such as the law applying to disputes between two states.

federal court. A court created by the U.S. Constitution or by Congress, having both diversity jurisdiction and federal-question jurisdiction.

federal-question jurisdiction. The exercise of federal-court authority over claims arising under the U.S. Constitution, an act of Congress, or a treaty. Cf. DIVERSITY JURISDICTION.

Federal Register. A daily publication in which U.S. administrative agencies publish their rules and regulations, including proposed rules and regulations for public comment.

fee. 1. A charge for labor or services, esp. professional services <a reasonable attorney's fee>. **2.** An inheritable interest in land, constituting maximal legal ownership; esp., a fee simple <Sarah received the land in fee>.

fee simple. An interest in land that endures until the current holder dies without heirs. ●

The fee simple is the broadest property interest allowed by law.—Often shortened to *fee*.

felony. A serious crime usu. punishable by imprisonment for more than one year or by death. ● Examples are murder, rape, arson, and burglary. Cf. MISDEMEANOR.

felony-murder rule. The doctrine holding that any death resulting from the commission or attempted commission of a felony is murder. ● Most states restrict this rule to inherently dangerous felonies such as rape, arson, robbery, or burglary.

fiat (**fee**-aht). [Latin "let it be done"] **1.** An order or decree, esp. an arbitrary one <judicial fiat>. **2.** A decree rendered by a court, esp. one relating to a routine matter such as scheduling <the fiat at the end of the motion set the date and time of the hearing>.

fiduciary (fi-**d[y]oo**-shee-er-ee), *n.* **1.** One who must exercise a high standard of care in managing another's money or property <the beneficiary sued the fiduciary for investing in speculative securities>.**2.** One who owes to another the duties of good faith, trust, confidence, and candor <the corporate officer is a fiduciary to the shareholders>.

fiduciary relationship. A relationship in which one person is under a duty to act for the benefit of the other on matters within the scope of the relationship. ● Fiduciary relationships—such as trustee-beneficiary, guardian-ward, agent-principal, and attorney-client—require the highest duty of care.

Fifth Amendment. The constitutional amendment, ratified with the Bill of Rights in 1791, providing that a person cannot be (1) required to answer for a capital or otherwise infamous offense unless a grand jury issues an indictment or presentment, (2) subjected to double jeopardy, (3) compelled to engage in self-incrimination, (4) deprived of life, liberty, or property without due process of law, and (5) deprived of private property for public use without just compensation.

file, *vb.* **1.** To deliver a legal document to the court clerk or record custodian for placement into the official record <the lawyer asked for an extension to file the reply brief>. **2.** To commence a lawsuit <Jon filed for divorce on Monday>.

finder of fact. See FACT-FINDER.

finding of fact. A determination by a judge, jury, or administrative agency of a fact supported by the evidence presented at the trial or hearing <at the conclusion of the bench trial, the judge made findings of fact and conclusions of law>.—Often shortened to *finding*. Cf. CONCLUSION OF LAW.

First Amendment. The constitutional amendment, ratified with the Bill of Rights in 1791, guaranteeing the freedoms of speech, religion, press, and assembly and the right to petition the government for the redress of grievances.

fixture. Personal property that has been attached to land or a building and that is regarded as an irremovable part of the real property, such as a fireplace built into a home. Cf. IMPROVEMENT.

force majeure (fors-mə-**zhoor** *or* -mah-**zhər**). [Law French "a superior force"] An event or effect that can be neither anticipated nor controlled. • The term *force majeure* includes acts of nature (such as floods or hurricanes) and acts of people (such as riots, strikes, or wars). Cf. ACT OF GOD.

forcible entry and detainer. A quick and simple legal proceeding for regaining possession of real property from someone who has wrongfully taken, or refused to surrender, possession.

foreclosure. A legal proceeding for the termination of a mortgagor's interest in property, instituted by the lender either to gain title or to force a sale in order to satisfy all or part of the unpaid debt secured by the property.

forfeiture (**for**-fi-chər). **1.** The divestiture of property without compensation. **2.** The loss of a right, privilege, or property because of a crime, breach of obligation, or neglect of duty. **3.** Something (esp. money or property) lost or confiscated by this process; a penalty.

forgery. 1. The act of fraudulently making a false document or altering a real one so that it may be used as if it were genuine <Clarence was charged with forgery of his grandmother's signature on her social-security check>. ● Though forgery was a misdemeanor at common law, modern statutes typically make it a felony. **2.** A false or altered document made to look genuine by someone with the intent to deceive <Richards was not the true property owner because the deed was a forgery>.

forum non conveniens (**for**-əm-non-kən-**veen**-ee-enz). [Latin "an unsuitable court"] In civil procedure, the doctrine that an inappropriate forum—even though competent under the law—may be divested of jurisdiction if, for the convenience of the litigants and the witnesses, it appears that the action should proceed in another forum in which the action might originally have been brought.

forum-shopping. The practice of choosing the most favorable jurisdiction or court in which a claim might be heard. ● For example, a plaintiff might engage in forum-shopping by filing suit in a jurisdiction with a reputation for high jury awards.

four-corners rule. 1. The principle that a document's meaning is to be gathered from the entire document and not from its isolated parts. **2.** The principle that no extraneous evidence should be considered when interpreting an unambiguous document. Cf. PAROL-EVIDENCE RULE.

Fourteenth Amendment. The constitutional amendment, ratified in 1868, whose primary provisions forbid states from denying due process and equal protection and from abridging the privileges and immunities of U.S. citizenship. ● The amendment also gives Congress the power to enforce these provisions, leading to such legislation as the Civil Rights Acts.

Fourth Amendment. The constitutional amendment, ratified with the Bill of Rights in 1791, prohibiting unreasonable searches and seizures and the issuance of warrants without probable cause.

franchise, *n.* **1.** The right to vote <the 19th Amendment gave women the franchise>. **2.** The right conferred by the government to engage in a certain business or to exercise corporate powers <the city put the cable-TV franchise rights up for bid>. **3.** The sole right granted by the owner of a trademark or tradename to engage in business or to sell a good or service in a certain area <Williamson bought a fast-food franchise>. **4.** The business or territory controlled by the person or entity that has been granted such a right <Frank's franchise was the only one in the city>.

fraud. 1. A knowing misrepresentation of the truth or concealment of a material fact to induce another to act to his or her injury. **2.** A misrepresentation made recklessly, without belief in its truth, to induce another person to act. **3.** A tort arising from a knowing misrepresentation, concealment of material fact, or reckless misrepresentation made to induce another to act to his or her detriment. **4.** Unconscionable dealing; esp., in contract law, the unconscientious use of the power arising out of the parties' relative positions and resulting in an unconscionable bargain.

fraudulent conveyance. A transfer of property for little or no consideration, made for the purpose of hindering or delaying a creditor by putting the property beyond the creditor's reach.

freedom of religion. The right to believe in any form of religion, to practice or exercise one's religious beliefs, and to be free from unreasonable governmental interference in one's religion, as guaranteed by the First Amendment.

freedom of speech. The right to express one's thoughts and opinions without unreasonable governmental restriction, as guaranteed by the First Amendment.

freedom of the press. The right to print and publish materials without governmental interference, as guaranteed by the First Amendment.

Free Exercise Clause. The constitutional provision (U.S. Const. amend. I) prohibiting the government from interfering in people's religious practices or forms of worship. Cf. ESTABLISHMENT CLAUSE.

friendly suit. A lawsuit in which all the parties have agreed beforehand to allow a court to resolve the issues involved. ● Friendly suits are often filed by settling parties who wish to have a judgment entered on the record.

friend of the court. See AMICUS CURIAE.

frivolous suit. A lawsuit having no legal basis, often filed to harass the defendant.

frustration. In contract law, the doctrine that, if the entire performance of a contract becomes fundamentally changed without any fault by either party, the contract is considered dissolved.—Also termed *frustration of purpose*. Cf. IMPOSSIBILITY (1).

Full Faith And Credit Clause. The constitutional provision (U.S. Const. art. IV, § 1) requiring states to recognize and enforce the legislative acts, public records, and judicial decisions of other states.

fundamental right. 1. A right derived from natural or fundamental law. **2.** In constitutional law, a right that triggers strict scrutiny of a law to determine whether the law violates the Due Process Clause or the Equal Protection Clause. ● Fundamental rights, as enunciated by the Supreme Court, include the right to vote, the right to interstate travel, and the various rights of privacy (such as marriage and contraception rights).

future interest. A property interest in which the privilege of possession or of enjoyment is future and not present. ● A future interest can exist in either the grantor (as with a reversion) or the grantee (as with a remainder or executory interest).—Also termed *future estate*.

G

gag order. A judge's order directing parties, attorneys, or witnesses to refrain from publicly discussing the facts of a case.

garnishee. A person or institution (such as a bank) that is indebted to or is bailee for another whose property has been subjected to garnishment.

garnisher. A creditor who initiates a garnishment action to reach the debtor's property that is thought to be held or owed to the debtor by a third party (the *garnishee*).—Also spelled *garnishor*.

garnishment. A judicial proceeding in which a creditor (or potential creditor) asks the court to order a third party who is indebted to or is bailee for the debtor to turn over to the creditor any of the debtor's property (such as wages or bank accounts) held by that third party. ● A plaintiff initiates a garnishment action as a means of either prejudgment seizure or postjudgment collection. Cf. ATTACHMENT; SEQUESTRATION (1).

general partnership. A partnership in which all partners participate fully in running the business and share equally in profits and losses, though the partners' monetary contributions may vary. Cf. LIMITED PARTNERSHIP.

gift tax. A tax imposed when property is voluntarily and gratuitously transferred. • Under federal law, the gift tax is imposed on the donor, while in some states it is imposed on the donee.

good faith. A state of mind consisting in (1) honesty in belief or purpose, (2) faithfulness to one's duty or obligation, (3) observance of reasonable commercial standards of fair dealing in a given trade or business, or (4) absence of intent to defraud or to seek unconscionable advantage. Cf. BAD FAITH.

goods. Tangible or movable personal property, esp. items of merchandise. • The sale of goods is governed by Article 2 of the UCC.

Good Samaritan law. A statute providing immunity from liability to a person (such as an off-duty doctor) who voluntarily renders aid to another in imminent danger but negligently causes injury while rendering the aid.

good time. A period deducted from a prisoner's sentence because of his or her good behavior while in prison.

grandfather clause. A statutory or regulatory clause that exempts a class of persons or transactions because of circumstances existing before the clause takes effect.

grand jury. A body of (often 23) people who are chosen to sit permanently for at least a month—and sometimes a year—and who, in ex parte proceedings, decide whether to issue indictments. ● If the grand jury decides that evidence is strong enough to hold a suspect for trial, it returns a bill of indictment (a *true bill*) charging the suspect with a specific crime.

grant, *vb.* **1.** To give or confer (a thing) with or without compensation <the parents granted the car to their daughter on her 16th birthday>. **2.** To formally transfer (real property) by deed <the Lewisons granted the townhouse to the Bufords>. **3.** To permit or agree to <the court granted the motion to dismiss>.

grantee. One to whom property is conveyed.

grantor. **1.** One who conveys property to another. **2.** The settlor of a trust.

gross negligence. **1.** A conscious, voluntary act or omission in reckless disregard of a legal duty and of the consequences to another party, who may typically recover punitive damages. **2.** Negligence so extreme that it is punishable as a crime. ● For example, involuntary manslaughter or other negligent homicide can be based on gross negligence, as when an extremely careless automobile driver kills someone.

guarantee, *n.* **1.** The act of giving security; the assurance that a contract or legal act will be duly carried out. **2.** Something given or existing as security to fulfill a future engagement or a condition subsequent.

guaranty, *n.* A promise to answer for someone else's debt, esp. in financial and banking contexts.

guardian. One who has the legal authority and duty of care for another's person or property, esp. because of the other's incapacity or disability. ● A guardian may be appointed either for all purposes or for specific purposes.

guardian ad litem (**gahr**-dee-ən-ad-lı-təm). A guardian, usu. a lawyer, appointed by the court to appear in a lawsuit on behalf of an incompetent or minor party. Cf. NEXT FRIEND.

H

habeas corpus (hay-bee-əs-**kor**-pəs). [Latin "you should have the body"] A writ employed to bring a person before a court, most frequently to ensure that the party's imprisonment is not illegal. ● In addition to being used to test the legality of an arrest or commitment, the writ may be used to obtain review of (1) the regularity of extradition process, (2) the right to or amount of bail, or (3) the jurisdiction of a court that has imposed a criminal sentence.—Also termed *writ of habeas corpus*.

headnote. A case summary that appears before the printed judicial opinion in a law report, addresses a point of law, and usu. includes the relevant facts bearing on that point of law.

hearing. A judicial or administrative session held for the purpose of deciding issues of fact or of law. ● At some hearings, evidence is presented; at others, only questions of law are argued.

hearsay. An assertion (either a verbal one or nonverbal assertive conduct), other than one made by the witness while testifying, offered in evidence to prove the truth of the matter asserted. ● Hearsay is inadmissible (except as provided otherwise by the rules of evidence) chiefly because out-of-court statements amounting to hearsay are not made under oath and are not subject to cross-examination.—Also termed *hearsay evidence*.

heat of passion. Rage, terror, or furious hatred suddenly aroused by some immediate provocation, usu. another person's words or actions. ● At common law, this could serve, in a murder defense, as a mitigating circumstance that would reduce the charge to manslaughter.

heir. 1. A person who, under the laws of intestacy, is entitled to receive an intestate decedent's property, esp. real property. **2.** Loosely, one who inherits real or personal property, whether by will or by intestate succession.

holder in due course. A person who in good faith has given value for a negotiable instrument that is complete and regular on its face, is not overdue, and, to the possessor's knowledge, has not been dishonored. ● Under the UCC, a holder in due course takes the instrument free of all claims and personal defenses, but subject to real defenses.

holding. 1. A determination of a matter of law that is pivotal to a judicial decision; a principle drawn from such a decision <the court's holding in *Plessy v. Ferguson* was overruled in *Brown v. Board of Education*>. Cf. DICTUM. **2.** A ruling on evidence or other questions presented at trial <the trial court's holding on competency prevented an insanity defense>. **3.** (*usu. pl.*) Property (esp. land) owned by a person <Jack put his holdings in a blind trust after he was elected>.

holdover tenant. A tenant who continues to occupy the leased premises after the lease has expired or has been legally terminated.

holographic will (ho-lə-**graf**-ik). A will that is entirely handwritten by the testator. • In many states, a holographic will is valid even if it is not witnessed.

homestead. The house, outbuildings, and adjoining land owned and occupied by a person or family as its principal residence. • As long as the homestead does not exceed in area or value the limits fixed by law, in most states it is exempt from forced sale for collection of a debt.

homicide (**ho**-mə-sɪd *or* **hoh**-). The killing of one person by another. See MURDER; MANSLAUGHTER.

honor, *vb.* To accept or pay (a negotiable instrument) when presented.

hornbook. A textbook containing the basic principles of an area of law. Cf. CASEBOOK.

hostile witness. A witness who is biased against the examining party or who is unwilling to testify. ● Hostile witnesses, unlike most other witnesses, may be asked leading questions on direct examination.

hung jury. A jury that cannot reach a verdict by the required voting margin.

I

id. *abbr.* [Latin *idem* "same"] The same. ● *Id.* is used in a legal citation to refer to the cited authority immediately preceding.

IFP. *abbr.* IN FORMA PAUPERIS.

immaterial, *adj.* Lacking any logical connection with the consequential facts; unimportant. Cf. IRRELEVANT.

immunity. 1. Any exemption from a duty, liability, or service of process; esp., such an exemption granted to a public official. **2.** In tort law, a doctrine providing a complete defense to a tort action. ● Unlike a privilege, immunity does not negate the tort, and it must be raised affirmatively or it will be waived. Cf. PRIVILEGE (2).

impeach, *vb.* **1.** To accuse (a public official) of a crime in office by presenting a written charge to an appropriate tribunal <Starr's supporters lobbied Congress to impeach the President>. **2.** To discredit the veracity of (a witness) <the prosecutor impeached the alibi witness with her prior conviction>. **3.** To challenge the accuracy or authenticity of (a document) <the plaintiff's deposition was used to impeach his affidavit>.

impleader. A procedure by which a third party is brought into a lawsuit, esp. by a defendant who seeks to shift liability to someone not sued by the plaintiff. Cf. INTERPLEADER; INTERVENTION.

implied, *adj.* Not directly stated or made known <implied consent> <an implied covenant>. Cf. EXPRESS.

implied-in-law contract. See QUASI-CONTRACT.

implied warranty. A warranty arising by operation of law because of the circumstances of a sale, rather than by the seller's express promise. Cf. EXPRESS WARRANTY.

impossibility. 1. In contract law, a fact or circumstance excusing performance because (1) the subject or means of performance has deteriorated, has been destroyed, or is no longer available, (2) the method of delivery or payment has failed, (3) a law now prevents performance, or (4) death or illness prevents performance.—Also termed *impossibility of performance*. Cf. FRUSTRATION. **2.** In criminal law, a fact or circumstance preventing the commission of a crime. ● Impossibility is a defense to the crime of attempt if what the defendant intended to do is not illegal, such as hunting while erroneously believing that it is

99

not hunting season (*legal impossibility*). Impossibility is not a defense to attempt when an act is illegal but cannot actually be accomplished, such as trying to pick an empty pocket (*factual impossibility*).

improvement. An addition to real property, whether permanent or not; esp., one that increases its value or utility or that enhances its appearance. Cf. FIXTURE.

inadmissible, *adj.* Not allowable or worthy of being admitted as evidence <the judge ruled that the opinion testimony was inadmissible>.

inalienable, *adj.* Incapable of being transferred or surrendered <inalienable rights>.

in camera. [Latin "in a chamber"] **1.** In the judge's private chambers.—Also termed *in chambers*. **2.** In the courtroom with all spectators excluded.

incapacity. Lack of ability to have certain legal consequences attach to one's actions; a legal disability.

inchoate (in-**koh**-ət), *adj.* **1.** Not yet completed or perfected <an inchoate lien>. **2.** Of or relating to a crime that is preliminary to another crime <attempt, solicitation, and conspiracy are inchoate offenses>.

incompetency. Lack of legal ability in some respect, esp. to stand trial or to testify <the defense lawyer established the child's incompetency to testify against her client>.

incorporation. 1. The formation of a legal corporation. See ARTICLES OF INCORPORATION. **2.** In constitutional law, the process of applying the provisions of the Bill of Rights to the states by interpreting the Fourteenth Amendment's Due Process Clause as encompassing those provisions.

incorporeal (in-kor-**por**-ee-əl), *adj.* Having a conceptual existence but no physical existence; intangible <copyrights and patents are incorporeal property>. Cf. CORPOREAL.

incriminate, *vb.* **1.** To charge (someone) with a crime <the grand jury incriminated the suspect>. **2.** To indicate (one's or another's) involvement in the commission of a crime or other wrongdoing <Gene incriminated himself when he couldn't explain his whereabouts on the night of the murder>. See SELF-INCRIMINATION.

indecent assault. See SEXUAL ASSAULT.

indecency. The quality or state of being offensive, esp. in a vulgar or sexual way. ● Unlike obscene material, indecent speech is protected under the First Amendment. Cf. OB-SCENITY.

indemnify, *vb.* **1.** To reimburse (another) for a loss suffered because of a third party's act or default. **2.** To promise to reimburse (another) for such a loss. **3.** To give security to (another) against such a loss.

indemnity (in-**dem**-nə-tee). **1.** A duty to make good any loss, damage, or liability another has incurred. **2.** The right of an injured party to claim reimbursement for its loss, damage, or liability from a person who has such a duty. **3.** Reimbursement or compensation for loss, damage, or liability. Cf. CONTRIBU-TION.

independent contractor. One who is hired to complete a specific project but who is left free to choose the methods for accomplishing the work. ● Unlike an employee, an independent contractor does not, upon committing a wrong while carrying out the work, create vicarious liability for an employer who did not authorize the wrongful act. Cf. EMPLOYEE.

indictment (in-**dīt**-mənt). **1.** The formal written accusation of a crime, affirmed by a grand jury and presented to a court for commencement of criminal proceedings against the accused. **2.** The act or process of preparing or bringing forward such a formal written accusation. Cf. INFORMATION.

indirect evidence. See CIRCUMSTANTIAL EVIDENCE.

indorsee (in-dor-**see**). One to whom a negotiable instrument is transferred by indorsement.—Also spelled *endorsee.*

indorsement. 1. The act of signing one's name on the back of a negotiable instrument in order to transfer it to someone else (esp. in return for the cash or credit value indicated on its face). **2.** The signature itself.—Also spelled *endorsement.*

indorser. One who transfers a negotiable instrument by indorsement.—Also spelled *endorser.*

ineffective assistance of counsel. In a criminal case, legal representation that is so faulty that the defendant is deprived of a fair trial. • The Supreme Court has held that ineffective assistance of counsel denies the defendant's Sixth Amendment right to counsel.

in forma pauperis (in-for-mə-**paw**-pər-əs). [Latin "in the manner of a pauper"] In the manner of an indigent who has permission to

103

disregard filing fees and court costs <after proving her indigency, Susan proceeded *in forma pauperis*>.—Abbr. IFP.

information. A formal criminal charge filed by a prosecutor without the involvement of a grand jury. • The information is used for prosecuting misdemeanors in most states. About half the states allow for it in felony prosecutions as well. Cf. INDICTMENT.

informed consent. A patient's agreement to medical treatment, made after a physician discloses whatever information a reasonably prudent physician in the medical community would provide to any patient about the risks involved in the treatment.

infra (**in**-frə). [Latin "below"] Later in this text. • *Infra* is used as a citational signal to refer to a subsequently cited authority. Cf. SUPRA.

infringement. An act that interferes with another's right or privilege, esp. an intellectual-property right such as a patent, copyright, or trademark.

inherit, *vb.* **1.** To receive (property) from an ancestor under the intestacy laws upon the ancestor's death. **2.** To receive (property) as a gift under a will.

inheritance tax. A tax imposed on a person who inherits property from another. ● There is no federal inheritance tax, but some states provide for one (though it is deductible under the federal estate tax). Cf. ESTATE TAX.

injunction. A court order commanding or preventing an action. ● To get an injunction, the complainant must show that there is no plain, adequate, and complete remedy at law and that an irreparable injury will result unless the relief is granted.

injury. 1. The violation of another's legal right, for which the law provides a remedy; a wrong or injustice. **2.** Harm or damage.

in personam (in-pər-**soh**-nəm), *adj.* [Latin "against a person"] Involving or determining the personal rights and interests of the parties. Cf. IN REM.

in re (in-ray *or* -ree), *prep.* [Latin "in the matter of"] (Of a judicial proceeding) not formally including adverse parties, but rather concerning something (such as an estate) <*In re Butler's Estate*>. ● The term is often used in case citations, esp. in uncontested proceedings.

in rem, *adj.* [Latin "against a thing"] Involving or determining the status of a thing, and

105

therefore the rights of persons generally with respect to that thing. Cf. IN PERSONAM.

insanity defense. In criminal law, an affirmative defense alleging that a mental disorder caused the accused to commit the crime. ● Most courts accept the insanity defense if the mental disorder prevented the person from knowing either the nature of the criminal act or whether the act was right or wrong. Unlike other defenses, a successful insanity defense results not in acquittal but instead in a special guilty verdict ("not guilty by reason of insanity") that usu. leads to the defendant's commitment to a mental institution.—Also termed *insanity plea*.

insolvency. 1. The state of one who cannot pay debts as they fall due or in the usual course of business. **2.** The inability to pay debts as they mature. See BANKRUPTCY.

instructed verdict. See DIRECTED VERDICT.

instrument. A formal legal document that entails rights, duties, entitlements, and liabilities, such as a contract, will, promissory note, or share certificate. See NEGOTIABLE INSTRUMENT.

insurance (in-**shuur**-əns). **1.** An agreement by which one party (the *insurer*) commits to do something of value for another party (the *in-*

sured) upon the occurrence of some specified contingency; esp., a contract by which the insurer, in exchange for a paid premium, agrees to indemnify or guarantee the insured against a loss caused by a specified event or risk. **2.** The sum for which something (as a person or property) is covered by such an agreement.

insurance policy. A contract of insurance; a document detailing such a contract.

intellectual property. 1. A category of intangible rights comprising primarily copyright, trademark, and patent law. **2.** A copyrightable work, a protectable trademark, or a patentable invention in which one has such intangible rights.

intent. The state of mind accompanying an act, esp. a forbidden act. ● While motive is the inducement to do some act, intent is the mental resolution or determination to do it. When the intent to do an act that violates the law exists, motive becomes immaterial. Cf. MOTIVE.

intentional infliction of emotional distress. The tortious offense of intentionally or recklessly causing a person to suffer severe emotional distress through one's extreme or outrageous acts. ● In a few states, a physical manifestation of the mental suffering is required.—Also termed *outrage*.

intentional tort. A tort committed by someone acting with general or specific intent. ● Examples are battery, false imprisonment, and trespass. Cf. NEGLIGENCE.

interest. 1. A legal claim or share in something <a property interest>. 2. The cost paid to a lender in return for the use of borrowed money <a high rate of interest>.

interlocutory (in-tər-**lok**-[y]ə-tor-ee), *adj.* (Of an order, judgment, appeal, etc.) temporary; not final in the determination of an action.

international law. The legal principles governing the relationships between nations; more modernly, the law of international relations, embracing not only nations but also such participants as international organizations, multinational corporations, nongovernmental organizations, and even individuals (such as those who invoke their human rights or commit war crimes).

interpleader. A suit to determine a matter of claim or right to property held by a usu. disinterested third party (called a *stakeholder*) who is in doubt about which claimant should have the property, and who therefore deposits the property with the court while the interested parties litigate over ownership. • Typically, a stakeholder initiates an interpleader both to determine which claimant should receive delivery or payment and to avoid multiple liability. Cf. IMPLEADER; INTERVENTION.

interrogatory (in-tə-**ro**-gə-tor-ee). Any one of a numbered list of written questions submitted in a legal context, usu. to an opposing party in a lawsuit as part of discovery.

intervention. 1. The entry into a lawsuit by a third party who, despite not being named a party to the action, has an interest in the outcome. • The intervenor sometimes joins the plaintiff in claiming what is sought, sometimes joins the defendant in resisting what is sought, and sometimes takes a position adverse to both the plaintiff and the defendant. Cf. IMPLEADER; INTERPLEADER. **2.** The legal procedure by which such a third party is allowed to become a party to the litigation.

inter vivos (in-tər-**vi**-vohs *or* -**vee**-vohs), *adj*. [Latin "between the living"] Of or relating to property conveyed not by will or in contemplation of an imminent death, but during the conveyor's lifetime <an inter vivos gift>.

109

intestacy (in-**tes**-tə-see). The fact or condition of a person's having died without a valid will. ● Each state has intestacy laws providing for the distribution of a decedent's estate to surviving relatives. Cf. TESTACY.

intestate, *adj.* **1.** Not having made a valid will <she died intestate>. **2.** Not disposed of by a will <intestate property>. **3.** Of or relating to intestacy <laws of intestate succession>.

invasion of privacy. An unjustified exploitation of one's personality or intrusion into one's personal activity, actionable under tort law and sometimes under constitutional law. ● The four types of invasion of privacy in tort are: (1) an appropriation, for one's benefit, of another's name or likeness, (2) an offensive, intentional interference with a person's seclusion or private affairs, (3) the public disclosure, of an objectionable nature, of private information about another, and (4) the use of publicity to place another in a false light in the public eye.

investigatory stop. See STOP AND FRISK.

invitee (in-vi-**tee**). One who has permission to enter or use another's premises, either as a business visitor or as a member of the public to whom the premises are held open. ● The occupier has a duty to inspect the premises

110

and to warn the invitee of nonobvious danger-ous conditions. Cf. LICENSEE (2).

involuntary manslaughter. Homicide in which there is no intention to kill or do griev-ous bodily harm, but that is committed with criminal negligence or during the commission of a misdemeanor or a felony not included within the felony-murder rule. Cf. VOLUNTARY MANSLAUGHTER.

irrebuttable presumption. See CONCLUSIVE PRESUMPTION.

irreconcilable differences. Persistent and unresolvable disagreements between spouses. ● Irreconcilable differences may be cited with-out specificity as grounds for a no-fault di-vorce.

irrelevant, *adj.* Not tending to prove or dis-prove a matter in issue; inapplicable. Cf. IMMA-TERIAL.

irrevocable (i-**rev**-ə-kə-bəl), *adj.* Unalterable; committed beyond recall <an irrevocable trust>.

issue, *n.* **1.** A material point in dispute <the court had to decide several complex issues>. **2.** Lineal descendants; offspring <the testator died without issue>.

J

JNOV. *abbr.* JUDGMENT NOTWITHSTANDING THE VERDICT.

joinder. The uniting of parties or claims in a single lawsuit.

joint and several liability. Liability that may be apportioned either among two or more parties or to only one or a few select members of the group, at the adversary's discretion. ● Thus, each liable party is individually responsible for the entire obligation, but a paying party has rights of contribution and indemnity against nonpaying parties.

joint tenancy. A tenancy with two or more coowners who take identical interests simultaneously by the same instrument and with the same right of possession. ● A joint tenancy differs from a tenancy in common because joint tenants each have a right of survivorship to the other's share. Cf. TENANCY IN COMMON.

joint venture. A business undertaking by two or more persons engaged in a single defined project, the necessary elements being: (1) an express or implied agreement; (2) a common purpose that the group intends to carry out; (3) shared profits and losses; and (4) each member's equal voice in controlling the project.—Also termed *joint adventure*; *joint enter-prise*. Cf. PARTNERSHIP.

J.P. *abbr*. JUSTICE OF THE PEACE.

judge, *n*. A public official appointed or elected to hear and decide legal matters in a court.—Abbr. J. (and, in plural, JJ.).

judgment. A court's final determination of the rights and obligations of the parties in a case <the judgment awarded the plaintiff $300,000>.

judgment lien. A lien imposed on the nonexempt property of a person against whom a judgment has been taken. See EXEMPT PROPERTY (1).

judgment notwithstanding the verdict. A judgment entered for one party even though a jury verdict has been rendered for the opposing party.—Also termed *judgment non obstante veredicto*.—Abbr. JNOV.

judgment-proof, *adj*. (Of an actual or potential judgment debtor) unable to satisfy a judgment for money damages because the person has no property, does not own enough property within the court's jurisdiction, or claims the benefit of statutorily exempt property <because the truck driver who caused the accident

113

was judgment-proof, the plaintiff sued the driver's employer instead>.

judicial notice. A court's acceptance, for purposes of convenience and without requiring a party's proof, of a well-known and indisputable fact; the court's power to accept such a fact <the trial court took judicial notice that a leap year has 366 days>.

judicial opinion. See OPINION (1).

judicial review. 1. A court's power to review the actions of other branches or levels of government; esp., the courts' power to invalidate legislative and executive actions as being unconstitutional. **2.** A court's review of a lower court's or an administrative body's factual or legal findings.

jurat (**juur**-at). [Latin *jurare* "to swear"] A certification added to an affidavit or deposition stating when and before what authority the affidavit or deposition was made. Cf. VERIFICATION.

jurisdiction. 1. A government's general power to exercise authority over all persons and things within its territory <Florida's jurisdiction>. **2.** A court's power to decide a case or issue a decree <long-arm jurisdiction>. **3.** A geographic area within which political or judicial authority may be exercised <the accused fled to another jurisdiction>. **4.** A political or judicial subdivision within such an area <other jurisdictions have decided the issue differently>. Cf. VENUE.

jurisprudence. 1. The study of the general or fundamental elements of a legal system, as opposed to its practical and concrete details; the philosophy of law <a law-school course in jurisprudence>. **2.** A system, body, or division of law <criminal jurisprudence>. **3.** A body of judicial opinions; judicial precedents considered collectively <California's jurisprudence>.

jury. A group of persons selected according to law and given the power to decide questions of fact and return a verdict in the case submitted to them.

jury charge. 1. A direction or guideline that a judge gives a jury concerning the law of the case.—Also termed *jury instruction*. **2.** A set of jury instructions.—Often shortened to *charge*.

jury panel. See VENIRE.

jury trial. A trial in which the factual issues are determined by a jury, not by the judge. Cf. BENCH TRIAL.

115

justice. 1. The fair and proper administration of laws <principles of equity, morality, and justice>. **2.** A judge, usu. an appellate judge <Justice Scalia wrote the majority opinion>.—Abbr. J. (and, in plural, JJ.).

justice of the peace. A local judicial officer having jurisdiction over minor criminal offenses and civil disputes, and authority to perform routine civil matters (such as administering oaths or performing marriage ceremonies).—Abbr. J.P. Cf. MAGISTRATE.

justifiable homicide. 1. The killing of another in self-defense when danger of death or serious bodily injury to the killer exists. See SELF-DEFENSE. **2.** A killing mandated or permitted by the law, such as execution for a capital crime or killing to prevent a crime or a criminal's escape.

justification. A legally sufficient reason for an act or omission that would otherwise be criminal or tortious; a showing of why a defendant did what the prosecution or plaintiff charges the defendant to answer for. ● An example of a justification in both criminal and tort law is self-defense. Cf. EXCUSE.

juvenile (**joo**-və-nəl *or* -nɪl), *n.* A person who has not reached the age (usu. 18) at which one is treated as an adult by the criminal-justice system; a minor.

juvenile delinquency. Antisocial behavior by a minor; esp., behavior that would be criminally punishable if the actor were an adult, but instead is usu. punished by special laws pertaining only to minors.

K

key-number system. A legal-research index-ing system developed by West Publishing Com-pany to catalogue American caselaw with headnotes. ● In this system, a number desig-nates a point of law, allowing a researcher to find all reported cases addressing a particular point by referring to its number.

kidnapping. The act or an instance of taking or carrying away a person without consent, by force or fraud, and without lawful excuse—and often with a demand for ransom (which, in most states, aggravates the offense).

L

labor union. See UNION.

laches (**lach**-iz). [Law French "remissness; slackness"] **1.** Unreasonable delay or negligence in pursuing a right or claim—almost always an equitable one—in a way that prejudices the party against whom relief is sought. **2.** The equitable doctrine by which courts deny relief to a claimant who has unreasonably delayed or been negligent in asserting the claim, when that delay or negligence has prejudiced the party against whom relief is sought.

landlord. One who leases real property to another.

lapse, *n.* **1.** The termination of a right or privilege because of neglect to exercise it within some time limit or because a contingency has not occurred <the seller said there was a lapse because the prospective buyer took too long to get a mortgage loan>. **2.** The failure of a gift in a will, esp. when the beneficiary dies before the testator dies <a lapse occurred because the husband died before the wife>.

larceny. The unlawful taking and carrying away of someone else's personal property with the intent to deprive the owner of it permanently. ● Grand larceny is larceny of property valued over a statutory amount (usu. $100).

law. 1. The regime that orders human activities and relations through systematic application of the force of politically organized society, or through social pressure, backed by force, in such a society; the legal system <the law of the land>. **2.** The aggregate of legislation, judicial precedents, and accepted legal principles; the body of authoritative grounds of judicial and administrative action <against the law>. **3.** The set of rules or principles dealing with a specific area of a legal system <the law of negligence>. **4.** A statute <a lemon law>.

law review. A journal containing scholarly articles, essays, and other commentary on legal topics by professors, judges, and practitioners. ● Law reviews are usu. published at law schools and edited by law students.

lawyer. One who is licensed to practice law.

lay witness. A witness who does not testify as an expert and who therefore may only give opinions or make inferences that are based on firsthand knowledge and helpful in understanding the testimony or in determining facts. Cf. EXPERT WITNESS.

leading case. 1. A judicial decision that first definitively settled an important legal rule or principle and that has since been often and consistently followed. ● An example is *Miranda v. Arizona*, 384 U.S. 436 (1966) (creating the exclusionary rule for evidence improperly obtained from a suspect being interrogated while in police custody). **2.** An important, often the most important, judicial precedent on a particular legal issue.

leading question. A question that suggests the answer to the person being asked; esp., a question that may be answered by a mere "yes" or "no." ● Leading questions are generally disallowed except in cross-examination.

lease, *n.* **1.** A temporary conveyance of the right to use and occupy real property, usu. in exchange for rent. ● The lease term can be for life, for a fixed period, or for a period terminable at will—but always for less time than the lessor has a right to. **2.** The written instrument memorializing the conveyance and its covenants. **3.** A temporary conveyance of personal property in exchange for consideration.

leave of court. Judicial permission to follow a nonroutine procedure <the plaintiff needed leave of court to file the amended complaint just before trial>.—Often shortened to *leave*.

legacy (**leg**-ə-see). A gift by will, esp. of personal property and often of money. Cf. BE-QUEST; DEVISE.

legal aid. Free or inexpensive legal services provided to those who cannot afford private counsel.

legal assistant. See PARALEGAL.

legal conclusion. A statement that expresses a legal duty or result but omits the facts creating or supporting the duty or result <the plaintiff's testimony that the defendant was negligent was an inadmissible legal conclusion>. Cf. CONCLUSION OF LAW.

legal description. A formal description of real property, including a description of any part subject to an easement or reservation, complete enough that a particular piece of land can be located and identified. ● The description can be made by reference to a government survey, metes and bounds, or lot numbers of a recorded plat.

legalese (lee-gə-**leez**). The jargon characteristically used by lawyers, esp. in legal documents.

legal ethics. The minimally acceptable standards of conduct within the legal profession, involving the duties that its members owe one another, their clients, and the courts.

legal owner. One recognized by law as the owner of something; esp., one (such as a trustee) who holds legal title to property for the benefit of another.

legal title. Title that evidences apparent ownership but does not necessarily signify full and complete title or a beneficial interest. Cf. EQUITABLE TITLE.

legislative history. The background and events leading to the enactment of a statute, including committee reports, hearings, and floor debates. ● Legislative history is usu. recorded so that it can later be used to aid in interpreting the statute.

lemon law. 1. A statute designed to protect consumers who buy substandard automobiles, usu. by requiring the manufacturer or dealer either to replace the vehicle or to refund the full purchase price. 2. Broadly, a statute designed to protect consumers who buy any products of inferior quality.

lessee (le-**see**). One who has a possessory interest in real or personal property under a lease; a tenant.

lesser included offense. A crime that is composed of some, but not all, of the elements of a more serious crime and that is necessarily committed in carrying out the greater crime <trespass is a lesser included offense of burglary>.

lessor (le-**sor** *or* **les**-or). One who conveys real or personal property by lease; a landlord.

letter of credit. An instrument under which the issuer (usu. a bank), at a customer's request, agrees to honor a draft or other demand for payment made by a third party (the *beneficiary*), as long as the draft or demand complies with specified conditions, and regardless of whether any underlying agreement between the customer and the beneficiary is satisfied. ● Letters of credit are governed by Article 5 of the UCC.

letter of intent. A noncommittal writing preliminary to a contract; a written statement detailing the preliminary understanding of parties who plan to enter into a contract or some other agreement.

letters of administration. A formal document issued by a probate court in order to appoint the administrator of an estate. See AD-MINISTRATION.

letters testamentary. The instrument by which a probate court approves the appointment of an executor under a will and authorizes the executor to administer the estate.

levy, *vb.* **1.** To impose or assess (a fine or a tax) by legal authority <levy a tax on cigarettes>. **2.** To take or seize property in execution of a judgment <the sheriff levied on the defendant's boat to satisfy the judgment>.

liability. 1. The quality or state of being legally obligated or responsible; the position of one who, by actual or threatened wrongdoing, is subjected to legal proceedings, whether criminal or civil in nature <the attorney wouldn't take the plaintiff's case because the hospital's liability was unlikely>. **2.** A pecuniary obligation; a debt <he filed for bankruptcy because his liabilities far exceeded his assets>.

liability insurance. An agreement to cover a loss resulting from one's liability to a third party, such as a loss incurred by a driver who injures a pedestrian.

libel (lɪ-bəl), *n.* A defamatory statement expressed in a tangible medium, esp. writing but also pictures, signs, or electronic broadcasts. See DEFAMATION. Cf. SLANDER.

license, *n.* **1.** A revocable permission to commit some act that would otherwise be unlawful <buyers must obtain a license before copying and distributing copyrighted software>. **2.** The certificate or document evidencing such permission <a hunting license>.

licensee. 1. One to whom a license is granted. **2.** One who has permission to enter or use another's premises, but only for his or her own purposes and not for the occupier's benefit (such as a social guest). ● The occupier has a duty to warn the licensee of any dangerous conditions known to the occupier but unknown to the licensee. Cf. INVITEE.

licensor. One who grants a license to another.

lie detector. See POLYGRAPH.

lien (leen *or* **lee**-ən *or* lin). A legal right or interest that a creditor has in another's property, lasting usu. until a debt or duty that it secures is satisfied. ● Typically, the creditor does not take possession of the property on which the lien has been obtained. Cf. PLEDGE.

life estate. An estate held only for the duration of a specified person's life, usu. the possessor's. ● Most life estates—created, for example, by a grant "to Jane for life"—are beneficial interests under trusts, the corpus being personal property, not real property.

limited-liability partnership. A partnership in which a partner is not liable for a negligent act committed by another partner or by an employee not under the partner's supervision. ● Almost half the states have enacted statutes that allow a business (typically a law firm or accounting firm) to register as this type of partnership.—Abbr. L.L.P.

limited partnership. A partnership composed of one or more persons who control the business and are personally liable for the partnership's debts (called *general partners*), and one or more persons who contribute capital and share profits but who cannot manage the business and are liable only for the amount of their contribution (called *limited partners*).— Abbr. L.P. Cf. GENERAL PARTNERSHIP.

lineup. A police identification procedure in which a criminal suspect and other physically similar persons are shown to the victim or a witness to determine whether the suspect can be identified as the criminal.

liquidated damages. An amount contractually stipulated as a reasonable estimation of actual damages to be recovered by one party if the other party breaches.

liquidation. 1. The act of determining by agreement or by litigation the exact amount of something (as a debt or damages) that before was uncertain. **2.** The act of settling a debt by payment or other satisfaction. **3.** The act of converting assets into cash, esp. for the purpose of settling debts. **4.** In bankruptcy law, the process—under Chapter 7 of the Bankruptcy Code—of collecting a debtor's nonexempt property, converting that property to cash, and distributing the cash to the various creditors.

lis pendens (lis-**pen**-dənz). [Latin "a pending lawsuit"] **1.** A pending litigation. **2.** The jurisdiction, power, or control acquired by a court over property during the pendency of a legal action. **3.** A notice required in some states to warn all persons that certain property is the subject matter of litigation, and that any interests acquired during the pendency of the suit are subject to the outcome of the litigation.

litigant. A party to a lawsuit.

litigation. 1. The process of carrying on a lawsuit <the costs of litigation force many

parties to settle>. **2.** A lawsuit itself <the litigation weighed heavily on the defendant>.

litigator. A trial lawyer, esp. one who handles mostly pretrial matters such as discovery.

living will. An instrument, signed with the formalities necessary for a will, by which a person states the intention to refuse medical treatment and to release healthcare providers from all liability if the person becomes both terminally ill and unable to communicate such a refusal.

L.L.P. *abbr.* LIMITED-LIABILITY PARTNERSHIP.

loan, *n.* **1.** An act of lending; a grant of something for temporary use <Trina gave him the laptop as a loan, not a gift>. **2.** A thing lent for the borrower's temporary use; esp., a sum of money lent at interest <Larry applied for a car loan>.

local rule. A rule by which an individual court supplements the procedural rules applying generally to all courts within the jurisdiction. ● Local rules deal with a variety of matters, such as requiring extra copies of motions to be filed with the court or prohibiting the reading of newspapers in the courtroom.

loitering. The criminal offense of remaining in a certain place (such as a public street) for no apparent reason. ● Loitering statutes are generally held to be unconstitutionally vague.

long-arm statute. A statute providing for the maintenance of jurisdiction over nonresident defendants who have had contacts with the state where the statute is in effect. ● Most state long-arm statutes extend this jurisdiction to its constitutional limits. See MINIMUM CONTACTS.

loss of consortium. A loss of the interests that one spouse is entitled to receive from the other, including companionship, cooperation, aid, affection, and sexual relations. ● Loss of consortium can be recoverable as damages in a personal-injury or wrongful-death action.

L.P. *abbr.* LIMITED PARTNERSHIP.

M

magistrate (**maj**-ə-strayt). A judicial officer with strictly limited jurisdiction and authority, often on the local level and often restricted to criminal cases. Cf. JUSTICE OF THE PEACE.

mailbox rule. In contract law, the rule that an acceptance becomes effective—and binds the offeror—once it is properly mailed. ● The mailbox rule does not apply, however, if the offer states that an acceptance is not effective until received.

maintenance. See ALIMONY.

majority opinion. An opinion joined in by more than half of the judges considering a given case, usu. on appeal.

maker. 1. A person who makes a promise in a promissory note by signing it. **2.** A drawer.

malice. 1. The intent, without justification or excuse, to commit a wrongful act. **2.** Reckless disregard of the law or of a person's legal rights.

malice aforethought. The requisite mental state for common-law murder, encompassing any one of the following: (1) the intent to kill, (2) the intent to inflict grievous bodily harm,

(3) extremely reckless indifference to the value of human life, or (4) the intent to commit a felony.

malicious prosecution. The tort of instituting criminal or civil proceedings for an improper purpose and without probable cause. ● The accused may sue for damages once the prosecution has been terminated in his or her favor.

malpractice. Negligence or incompetence on the part of a professional (such as a doctor or lawyer).

mandamus (man-**day**-məs). [Latin "we command"] A writ issued by a superior court compelling a lower court or a public body or officer to perform a mandatory or purely ministerial duty.—Also termed *writ of mandamus*.

manslaughter. The unlawful killing of a human being without malice aforethought. See MALICE AFORETHOUGHT. Cf. MURDER.

marital privilege. 1. The privilege allowing a spouse not to testify about confidential communications made with the other spouse during the marriage.—Also termed *marital-communications privilege*. **2.** The privilege allowing a spouse not to testify in a criminal case as an adverse witness against the other spouse, regardless of the subject matter of the testimony.

marital property. Property that is acquired from the time when a marriage begins until one spouse files for divorce (assuming a divorce decree actually results). See COMMUNITY PROPERTY.

maritime court. See ADMIRALTY (1).

maritime law. The body of law governing marine commerce and navigation, the transportation at sea of persons and property, and marine affairs in general; the rules governing contract, tort, and workers'-compensation claims arising out of commerce on or over water.—Also termed *admiralty*; *admiralty law*. See ADMIRALTY.

mark, *n*. See TRADEMARK.

marriage. The legal union of a man and woman as husband and wife. ● Most states require a marrying couple to obtain a marriage license and have a wedding ceremony conducted by a clergy member or public official. Cf. COMMON-LAW MARRIAGE.

martial law. A body of rules applied on grounds of necessity by a country's rulers when the civil government has failed or ap-

pears as if it might fail to function. ● The
military assumes control and enforces these
rules purportedly until the civil government
can be restored. Cf. MILITARY LAW.

master, *n*. A parajudicial officer (such as a
referee, auditor, examiner, or assessor) special-
ly appointed to help a court with its proceedings. ● Among the functions a master may
perform are taking testimony, computing interest, valuing annuities, investigating encumbrances on land titles, and the like—virtually
always with a written report to the court.

material, *adj*. **1.** Having some logical connection with the consequential facts <material
evidence>. **2.** Of such a nature that knowledge
of the item would affect a person's decision-
making process; significant; essential <a material representation>.

matter. 1. A subject under consideration, esp.
involving a dispute or litigation; a case <the
matter before the court was complex>. **2.**
Something that is to be tried or proved; an
allegation forming the basis of a claim or defense <the jury decides only factual matters>.

mechanic's lien. A statutory lien that secures payment for labor or materials supplied
in improving, repairing, or maintaining real or

personal property (such as a building or auto-mobile).

mediation. A method of nonbinding dispute resolution involving a neutral third party who tries to help the disputing parties reach a mutually agreeable solution. Cf. ARBITRATION.

Megan's law. A statute requiring local au-thorities to notify communities of the where-abouts of convicted sex offenders who have been released from prison. ● All states have these laws, but only some require community notification (as by publishing offenders' pic-tures or addresses in local newspapers); in others, people must call a state hotline or submit names of persons they suspect.

memorandum. 1. An informal written note or record outlining the terms of a transaction or contract <the buyer's memorandum listed the price of the goods at $7,000>. See STATUTE OF FRAUDS. **2.** A party's written statement of its legal arguments presented to the court, usu. in the form of a brief <a memorandum of law accompanied the motion to dismiss>.

mens rea (menz-**ray**[-ə] *or* -**ree**-ə). [Law Lat-in "guilty mind"] The state of mind that the prosecution, to secure a conviction, must prove that a defendant had when committing a crime; criminal intent or recklessness <the *mens rea* for murder is intent to kill>. • *Mens rea* is the second of two essential elements of every crime at common law, the other being *actus reus*. Cf. ACTUS REUS.

mental anguish. See EMOTIONAL DISTRESS.

merger. The absorption of one company (esp. a corporation) that ceases to exist into another that retains its own name and identity and acquires the assets and liabilities of the former. • Corporate mergers must conform to statutory formalities and usu. must be approved by a supermajority of shareholders.

merger clause. A contractual provision stating that the contract represents the parties' complete and final agreement and supersedes all informal understandings and oral agreements relating to the subject matter of the contract. See PAROL-EVIDENCE RULE.

merits. The elements or grounds of a claim or defense; the substantive considerations to be taken into account in deciding a case, as opposed to extraneous or technical points, esp. of procedure <trial on the merits>.

metes and bounds. The territorial limits of real property as measured by distances and angles from designated landmarks and in relation to adjoining properties. ● Metes and bounds are usu. described in deeds and surveys to establish the boundary lines of land.

military law. The branch of public law governing military discipline and other rules regarding service in the armed forces. ● Military law is exercised both in peacetime and in war, and is recognized by civil courts. Cf. MARTIAL LAW.

mineral right. The right to search for, develop, and remove minerals from land or to receive a royalty based on the production of minerals.

minimum contacts. A nonresident defendant's forum-state connections, such as business activity or actions foreseeably leading to business activity, that are substantial enough to bring the defendant within the forum-state court's personal jurisdiction without offending traditional notions of fair play and substantial justice.

minor, *n.* A person who has not reached full legal age; a child or juvenile.

***Miranda* rule.** The requirement that a criminal suspect in police custody must be informed of certain constitutional rights before being interrogated. ● The suspect must be warned of the right to remain silent, the right to have an attorney present during questioning, and the right to have an attorney appointed if the suspect cannot afford one. If the person is not advised of these rights or does not validly waive them, any evidence obtained in the interrogation cannot be used against the defendant at trial. *Miranda v. Arizona*, 384 U.S. 436 (1966).

misdemeanor (mis-də-**mee**-nər). A crime that is less serious than a felony and is usu. punishable by fine, penalty, forfeiture, or confinement in a place other than prison (such as a county jail). Cf. FELONY.

misrepresentation. A false or misleading statement about something, usu. with the intent to deceive. See FRAUD.

mistake of fact. An erroneous belief about a fact that is material to a transaction.

mistake of law. An erroneous belief about the legal effect of a known fact or situation.

mistrial. A trial that ends without a determination on the merits because of prejudicial error or misconduct or because of a hung jury <because several jurors discussed the case with outsiders, the judge declared a mistrial>.

mitigation-of-damages doctrine. The principle requiring a plaintiff, after an injury or breach of contract, to use ordinary care to alleviate the effects of the injury or breach. ● If the defendant can show that the plaintiff failed to mitigate damages, the plaintiff's recovery can be reduced.

mock trial. A fictitious trial organized to allow law students, or sometimes lawyers, to practice the techniques of trial advocacy. Cf. MOOT COURT.

monopoly. 1. Control or advantage obtained by one supplier or producer over the commercial market within a given region. **2.** The market condition existing when only one economic entity produces a particular product or provides a particular service. ● The term is now commonly applied also to situations that approach but do not strictly meet this definition.

moot, *adj.* Having no practical significance; hypothetical or academic <a court will not decide a moot issue>.

moot court. A fictitious court held usu. in law schools to argue hypothetical cases, esp. at the appellate level. Cf. MOCK TRIAL.

moral turpitude. Conduct that is contrary to justice, honesty, or good morals. ● In the area of legal ethics, offenses involving moral turpitude—such as fraud or breach of trust—traditionally make a person unfit to practice law.

mortgage (**mor**-gij). **1.** A conveyance of real estate or some real-estate interest, voidable upon the payment of money or the performance of some other condition. **2.** A lien or charge on specific property (usu. real property) created by a document that purports to be an express transfer of title, with or without possession, but accompanied by a condition that the transfer will become void if money owed for the property is not paid in a timely fashion or the thing done to secure the transfer is not performed. **3.** An instrument (such as a deed of trust or contract) specifying the terms of such a transaction.

mortgagee (mor-gə-**jee**). One to whom property is mortgaged; the mortgage-creditor, or lender.

mortgagor (mor-gə-**jor**). One who mortgages property; the mortgage-debtor, or borrower.

motion. A written or oral application requesting a court to make a specified ruling or order <a motion to dismiss>.

motion for new trial. A postjudgment request that the court vacate the judgment and order a new trial for any of various reasons, such as insufficient evidence, newly discovered evidence, or jury misconduct. ● In many states, this motion is required before a party can file an appeal.

motion for summary judgment. A request that the court enter judgment without a trial because there is no genuine issue of material fact in the case and because the movant is entitled to prevail as a matter of law. See SUM-MARY JUDGMENT.

motion in limine (**lim**-i-nee). A pretrial request that certain inadmissible evidence not be referred to or offered before the jury. ● Typically, a party makes this motion when it believes that mere mention of the evidence during trial would be highly prejudicial and could not be remedied by an instruction to disregard.

motion to suppress. A request that the court prohibit the introduction of illegally obtained evidence at a criminal trial. See EXCLUSIONARY RULE.

motive. Something, esp. willful desire, that causes one to act. Cf. INTENT.

movant (**moo**-vənt). One who makes a motion to the court <the judge asked the movant to argue first, then the respondent>.

municipal corporation. A city, town, or other local political entity formed by charter from the state and having the autonomous authority to administer the state's local affairs.—Also termed *municipality*.

muniment of title. Documentary evidence of title, such as a deed or a judgment regarding the ownership of property. See CHAIN OF TITLE.

murder, *n.* The unlawful killing of a human being with malice aforethought. • The statutory elements of murder vary from state to state. Most penal codes divide the crime into two or more degrees of severity and punishment. See MALICE AFORETHOUGHT. Cf. MANSLAUGHTER.

mutual mistake. An erroneous belief shared and relied upon by both parties to a contract. • A court will often revise or void a contract based on a mutual mistake about a material term. Cf. UNILATERAL MISTAKE.

N

natural-death act. A statute that allows a person to issue a written directive instructing a physician to withhold life-sustaining procedures if the person is terminally ill. See LIVING WILL.

natural law. A philosophical system of legal and moral principles purportedly deriving from a universalized conception of human nature or divine justice rather than from legislative or judicial action; moral law embodied in principles of right and wrong. Cf. POSITIVE LAW.

necessity. **1.** In criminal law, a justification defense for a person who acts in an emergency that he or she did not create and who commits a harm that is less severe than the harm that would have occurred but for the person's actions. ● For example, a mountain climber can assert necessity as a defense to theft if, while lost in a blizzard, he takes food and blankets from another's cabin. **2.** In tort law, a privilege that may relieve a person from liability if that person, having no alternative, harms another's property to protect life or health.

negligence. **1.** The failure to exercise the standard of care that a reasonably prudent person would have exercised in the same situation; any conduct that falls below the legal standard established to protect others against unreasonable risk of harm, except for conduct that is intentionally, wantonly, or willfully disregardful of others' rights. **2.** A tort grounded in this failure, usu. expressed in terms of the following elements: duty, breach of duty, causation, and damages.

negligence per se. Negligence established as a matter of law, so that breach of the duty is not a jury question. ● Negligence per se usu. arises from a statutory violation, such as speeding or running a red light.

negligent entrustment. The act of leaving a dangerous article (such as a gun or car) with a person who the lender knows or should know is likely to use it in an unreasonably risky manner <the parents were sued for negligent entrustment because they let their 12–year-old drive their minivan>.

negligent homicide. Homicide resulting from the careless performance of a legal or illegal act in which the danger of death is apparent; the killing of a human being by criminal negligence.

negotiable instrument. A written instrument that (1) is signed by the maker or drawer, (2) includes an unconditional promise or order to pay a specified sum of money, (3) is payable on demand or at a definite time, and (4) is payable to order or to bearer. ● The most common types of negotiable instruments are notes and drafts.

next friend. A person who appears in a lawsuit on behalf of an incompetent or minor plaintiff, but who is not a party to the lawsuit and is not appointed as a guardian. Cf. GUARDIAN AD LITEM.

no bill, *n.* A grand jury's notation that insufficient evidence exists for an indictment on a criminal charge <the grand jury returned a no bill, so the suspect was released>. Cf. TRUE BILL.

no contest. A criminal defendant's plea that, while not admitting guilt, the defendant will not dispute the charge <Laura pleaded no contest to the speeding ticket>. ● This plea is often preferable to a guilty plea, which can be used against the defendant in a later civil lawsuit.—Also termed *nolo contendere*.

no-contest clause. A testamentary provision stating that a named beneficiary forfeits any gift granted by the will if he or she challenges the will.

no-fault divorce. A divorce in which the parties are not required to prove fault or grounds beyond a showing of the irretrievable breakdown of the marriage or irreconcilable differences.

nolo contendere. See NO CONTEST.

noncompetition clause. A contractual provision—typically found in employment, partnership, or sale-of-business agreements—in which one party agrees to refrain from conducting business similar to that of the other party. • Courts usu. uphold these clauses for the duration of the orig;nal business relationship, but clauses extending beyond termination must usu. be reasonable in scope, time, and territory.—Also termed *noncompete clause*; *covenant not to compete*; *restrictive covenant*.

non compos mentis (non-kom-pəs-**men**-təs), *adj.* [Latin "not master of one's mind"] Insane or mentally incompetent.

nonjury trial. See BENCH TRIAL.

nonmovant. A litigating party other than the one that has filed a motion currently under consideration. Cf. MOVANT.

nonprofit corporation. A corporation organized under special statutes for some purpose other than making a profit, and therefore afforded special tax treatment.—Also termed *not-for-profit corporation*.

nonsuit. 1. A plaintiff's voluntary dismissal of a case or of a defendant. **2.** A court's dismissal of a case or of a defendant because the plaintiff has failed to make out a legal case or to bring forward sufficient evidence.

notary public (**noh**-də-ree). A person authorized by a state to administer oaths, certify documents, attest to the authenticity of signatures, and perform official acts in commercial matters, such as protesting negotiable instruments.—Often shortened to *notary*.

note, *n.* A written promise by one party (the *maker*) to pay money to another party (the *payee*) or to bearer. • A note is a two-party negotiable instrument, unlike a draft (which is a three-party instrument).—Also termed *promissory note*. Cf. DRAFT.

not-for-profit corporation. See NONPROFIT CORPORATION.

notice, *n.* **1.** Legal notification required by law or agreement, or imparted by operation of law as a result of some fact (such as the recording of instruments); definite legal cognizance, actual or constructive, of an existing

147

right or title <under the lease, the tenant must give the landlord written notice 30 days before vacating the premises>. **2.** The condition of being so notified, whether or not actual awareness exists <the buyer was on notice because the lien was on the car's title>.

novation (noh-**vay**-shən). The substitution for an old contract a new one that either replaces an existing obligation with a new obligation or replaces an original party with a new party.

nuisance. A condition or situation (such as a loud noise or foul odor) that interferes with another's use or enjoyment of property. • If the interference is substantial and unreasonable, the responsible party may be held liable in tort. Cf. ATTRACTIVE NUISANCE.

nuncupative will (nən-**kyoo**-pə-tiv *or* nəng-kyə-pay-div). An oral will made in contemplation of imminent death from an injury recently incurred. • Nuncupative wills are invalid in most states, but in those states allowing them, the amount that may be conveyed is usu. limited by statute, and they traditionally apply only to personal property.

O

oath. **1.** A solemn pledge by which the person swearing to a statement implicitly invites punishment from a supreme being if the person is untruthful. **2.** A statement made after making such a pledge. Cf. AFFIRMATION.

obiter dictum. See DICTUM.

objection. A formal statement protesting something that has occurred in court and seeking the judge's immediate ruling on the point. ● The person objecting must usu. state the basis for the objection to preserve the right to appeal an adverse ruling.

objective standard. A legal standard that is based on conduct and perceptions external to a particular person. ● In tort law, for example, the reasonable-person standard is considered an objective standard because it does not require a determination of what the defendant was thinking. Cf. SUBJECTIVE STANDARD.

obscenity. **1.** The quality or state of being morally abhorrent or socially taboo, esp. as a result of referring to or depicting sexual or excretory functions. ● Under the Supreme Court's three-part test, material is legally obscene—and therefore not protected under the First Amendment—if, taken as a whole, the material (1) appeals to the prurient interest in sex, as determined by the average person applying contemporary community standards; (2) portrays sexual conduct, as specifically defined by the applicable state law, in a patently offensive way; and (3) lacks serious literary, artistic, political, or scientific value. **2.** Something (such as an expression or act) that has this quality. Cf. INDECENCY.

obstruction of justice. Interference with the orderly administration of law (such as by withholding evidence or intimidating a witness). • Obstruction of justice is a crime in most states.

offense. A violation of the law; a crime, often a minor one.

offer, *n.* **1.** The act or an instance of presenting something for acceptance <a prosecutor's offer of a plea bargain>. **2.** A promise to do or refrain from doing some specified thing in the future; a display of willingness to enter into a contract on specified terms, made in a way that would lead a reasonable person to understand that an acceptance, having been sought, will result in a binding contract <an offer to buy a house>. Cf. ACCEPTANCE.

officer of the court. A person who is charged with upholding the law and the judicial system. ● Typically, *officer of the court* refers to a judge, clerk, bailiff, sheriff, or the like, but the term also applies to a lawyer, who is obliged to obey court rules and who owes a duty of candor to the court.

omission. **1.** A failure to do something; a neglect of duty <the complaint alleged that the driver committed various negligent acts and omissions>. **2.** The act of leaving something out; a thing left out <the omission of the sales price rendered the contract void>.

opening statement. At the outset of a trial, an advocate's statement giving the fact-finder a preview of the case and of the evidence to be submitted.—Also termed *opening argument.*

operation of law. The means by which a right or a liability is created for a party regardless of the party's actual intent <because the court didn't rule on the motion for rehearing within 30 days, it was overruled by operation of law>.

opinion. **1.** A court's written statement explaining its decision in a given case, including the statement of facts, points of law, rationale, and dicta <the supreme court disapproved the lower court's opinion>.—Also termed *judicial opinion.* **2.** A formal expression of judgment or advice based on an expert's special knowledge; esp., a document, usu. prepared at a client's request, containing a lawyer's understanding of the law that applies to a particular case <the insurance company asked for a coverage opinion>.—Also termed *opinion letter*. **3.** A witness's thoughts, beliefs, or inferences about facts in dispute, as opposed to personal knowledge of the facts themselves <the judge would not allow the witness to give her opinion on the defendant's guilt>.

option. 1. A contract made to keep an offer open for a specified period, so that the offeror cannot revoke the offer during that period <the option is valid because it is supported by consideration>.—Also termed *option contract*. **2.** The right conveyed by such a contract <Bob didn't exercise his first option to buy the house>. **3.** The right (but not the obligation) to buy or sell a given quantity of securities, commodities, or other assets at a fixed price within a specified time <trading stock options is a speculative business>.

oral argument. An advocate's spoken presentation before a court (esp. an appellate court) supporting or opposing the legal relief at issue.

order, *n.* **1.** A written direction or command delivered by a court or judge.—Also termed *court order.* **2.** A written direction to pay money or deliver property to a specified person.

ordinance. A statute or regulation, esp. one enacted by a city government <a zoning ordinance>.

outrage. See INTENTIONAL INFLICTION OF EMOTIONAL DISTRESS.

overrule, *vb.* **1.** To rule against; to reject <the judge overruled the plaintiff's objection>. **2.** (Of an appellate court) to overturn or set aside (a precedent) by expressly deciding it should no longer be controlling law <in *Casey*, the Supreme Court chose not to overrule *Roe v. Wade*>.

owner. One who has the right to possess, use, and convey something; a proprietor.

P

pain and suffering. Physical discomfort or emotional distress compensable as an element of damages in torts <the jury awarded the plaintiff $50,000 for past pain and suffering>.

panel. 1. A group of persons selected for jury duty; a venire. **2.** A set of judges selected from a complete court to decide a specific case; esp., a group of three judges designated to sit for an appellate court.

paper. See COMMERCIAL PAPER.

paralegal. A person who assists a lawyer in duties related to the practice of law, but who is not a trained or licensed attorney.—Also termed *legal assistant*.

pardon, *n.* The act or an instance of officially nullifying punishment or other legal consequences of a crime. ● A pardon is usu. granted by the chief executive, such as the President (for federal crimes) or a governor (for state crimes).

parol (**par-**əl *or* pə-**rohl**), *adj.* **1.** Oral; unwritten <parol evidence>. **2.** Not under seal <parol contract>.

parole (pə-**rohl**), *n.* The release of a prisoner from imprisonment before the full sentence has been served. ● Although not available under some sentences, parole is usu. granted for good behavior on the condition that the parolee regularly report to a parole officer for a specified period.

parol-evidence rule. In contract law, the principle that a writing intended by the parties to be a final embodiment of their agreement cannot be modified by evidence that adds to, varies, or contradicts the writing. ● This rule usu. prevents a party from introducing extrinsic evidence of negotiations that occurred before or while the agreement was being reduced to its final written form.

partner. 1. One who shares or takes part with another, esp. in a venture with shared benefits and shared risks; an associate or colleague <partners in crime>. 2. One of two or more persons who jointly own and carry on a business for profit <the law firm has three partners>.

partnership. A voluntary association of two or more persons who jointly own and carry on a business for profit. ● A partnership is usu. presumed to exist if the persons agree to proportionally share the business's profits or losses. Cf. JOINT VENTURE.

party. A person involved in a legal transaction or court proceeding <a party to the lease> <a party to the lawsuit>.

patent (**pat**-[ə]nt), *n.* **1.** The governmental grant of a right, privilege, or authority; the official document so granting. **2.** The exclusive right to make, use, or sell an invention for a specified period (usu. 17 years), granted by the federal government to the inventor if the device or process is novel, useful, and nonobvious.

paternity suit. A court proceeding to determine whether a person is the father of a child born out of wedlock, usu. initiated by the mother in an effort to obtain child support.

pawn, *n.* **1.** An item of personal property deposited as security for payment of a debt; a pledge or guarantee. **2.** The act of depositing personal property in this manner. **3.** The condition of being held on deposit as a pledge.

payee. One to whom money is paid or payable; esp., a party named in a negotiable instrument as the recipient of the payment.

payment. 1. Performance of an obligation, usu. by the delivery of money. ● Performance may occur by delivery and acceptance of things other than money, but there is a payment only if money or other valuable things are given and accepted in partial or full discharge of an obligation. **2.** The money or other valuable thing so delivered in satisfaction of an obligation.

payor. One who pays; esp., a person responsible for paying a negotiable instrument. See DRAWEE.

P.C. *abbr.* PROFESSIONAL CORPORATION.

P.D. *abbr.* PUBLIC DEFENDER.

pecuniary (pə-**kyoo**-nee-er-ee), *adj.* Of or relating to money; monetary <the doll, though rare, had no significant pecuniary value>.

penal code. A compilation of a state's criminal laws, usu. categorizing the offenses and their respective punishments.

penalty. 1. Punishment imposed on a wrongdoer, esp. in the form of imprisonment or fine. • Though usu. for crimes, penalties are also sometimes imposed for civil wrongs. **2.** Excessive liquidated damages that a contract purports to impose on a party that breaches. • If the damages are excessive enough to be considered a penalty, a court will usu. not enforce that particular provision of the contract. Some contracts specify that a given sum of damages is intended "as liquidated damages and not as a penalty"—but even that language is not foolproof.

per capita (pər-**ka**-pi-tə), *adv. or adj.* [Latin "by the head"] Divided equally among all individuals, usu. in the same class <the probate court divided the estate among the children per capita>. Cf. PER STIRPES.

per curiam opinion. An opinion handed down by an appellate court without identifying the individual judge who wrote the opinion.—Sometimes shortened to *per curiam*.

peremptory challenge. One of a party's limited number of requests to remove a potential juror from the jury panel. ● A peremptory challenge need not be supported by any reason unless the opposing party objects that the challenge was made for the purpose of discriminating on the basis of race or sex.—Often shortened to *peremptory*.

perfect (pər-**fekt**), *vb.* To take all legal steps needed to complete, secure, or record (a claim, right, or interest); to put in final conformity with the law <perfect a security interest> <perfect an appeal>.

performance. 1. The successful completion of a contractual duty, usu. resulting in the performer's release from any past or future liability. **2.** The equitable doctrine by which acts consistent with an intention to fulfill an obligation are construed to be in fulfillment of that obligation, even if the party was silent on the point.

periodic tenancy. A tenancy that automatically continues for successive periods (usu. month to month or year to year) unless terminated at the end of a period by notice. ● A typical example is a month-to-month apartment lease.

perjury (pər-jər-ee). The crime of deliberately giving false or misleading testimony while under oath or affirmation.

per se (pər-**say**), *adj. or adv.* [Latin] **1.** Of, in, or by itself; standing alone, without reference to additional facts <the price-fixing agreement violates antitrust law per se>. **2.** As a matter of law <negligence per se>.

personal injury. 1. In a tort action for negligence, any harm caused to a person, such as a broken bone, a cut, or a bruise; bodily injury. **2.** Any invasion of personal rights, including mental suffering and false imprisonment. **3.** In workers'-compensation law, any harm (including a worsened preexisting condition) that arises in the scope of employment.

personal jurisdiction. A court's power to bring persons into its adjudicative process; jurisdiction over a defendant's personal rights, rather than merely over property interests. Cf. SUBJECT-MATTER JURISDICTION.

personal knowledge. An awareness or understanding of a fact or condition acquired by a person directly through his or her own senses, as opposed to learning from some other person or source.

personal property. Any movable or intangible thing that is subject to ownership and not classified as real property.—Also termed *personalty*. Cf. REAL PROPERTY.

per stirpes (pər-**stər**-peez), *adv. or adj.* [Latin "by roots or stocks"] Proportionally divided between beneficiaries according to their deceased ancestor's share <because several children had died before their mother did, the court made a per stirpes distribution to the heirs>. Cf. PER CAPITA.

petition, *n.* **1.** A formal written request presented to a court or other official body. **2.** In some states, a lawsuit's first pleading; a complaint.

petitioner. A party who makes a petition to a court or other official body. Cf. RESPONDENT.

petit jury. A jury (usu. consisting of 12 persons) summoned, empaneled, and participating in the trial of a specific case; a trial jury, as opposed to a grand jury.

piercing the corporate veil. The judicial act of imposing personal liability on otherwise immune corporate officers, directors, or shareholders for a corporation's fraudulent or wrongful acts.

plain-meaning rule. A principle of interpretation prohibiting the examination of any information not contained in a contract, statute, or other document being considered; esp., the statutory-interpretation rule requiring the application of a word's obvious and customary meaning, without analyzing legislative intent.

plaintiff. The party who brings a civil suit in a court of law. Cf. DEFENDANT.

plea. 1. An accused person's formal response to a criminal charge <a plea of no contest>. **2.** In civil litigation, an allegation or pleading made in response to a claim <a plea in abatement>.

161

plea bargain, *n*. An agreement between the prosecutor and criminal defendant to resolve a case without trial, usu. allowing the defendant to plead guilty to a lesser offense or testify against another in return for a less severe punishment.

plead, *vb*. **1.** To make a specific plea <he pleaded not guilty>. **2.** To assert or allege in a pleading <fraud claims must be pleaded with particularity>. **3.** To file or deliver a pleading <the plaintiff hasn't pleaded yet>.

pleading. A document containing the factual allegations that each party is required to communicate to the opponent before trial. ● In federal civil procedure, the main pleadings are the plaintiff's complaint and the defendant's answer.

plea in abatement. A plea that objects to the place, time, or method of asserting the plaintiff's claim but does not dispute the claim's merits. ● A defendant who successfully asserts a plea in abatement leaves the claim open for continuation in the current action or reassertion in a later action if the defect is cured.

plea in bar. A plea that seeks to defeat the plaintiff's or prosecutor's action completely and permanently.

pledge, *n.* **1.** A bailment or other deposit of personal property to a creditor as security for a debt or obligation; a pawn. Cf. LIEN. **2.** The item of personal property so deposited; a pawned item. **3.** Broadly, the act of providing something as security for a debt or obligation; the thing so provided.

plurality opinion. An opinion lacking enough judges' votes to constitute a majority, but receiving more votes than any other opinion.

pocket part. A supplemental pamphlet inserted usu. into the back inside cover of a lawbook (esp. a treatise or code) to update the material in the main text until the publisher issues a new edition of the book <the pocket part contained the amended version of the statute>.

point of error. A mistake by a lower court asserted as a ground for appeal. See ERROR.

police power. A state's constitutional right to establish and enforce laws protecting the public's health, safety, and general welfare, or to delegate this right to local governments. ● A state's police power is subject to constitutional limitations such as due process and the supremacy of federal law.

polygraph. A device used to evaluate a person's truthfulness by measuring and recording involuntary physiological changes in the human body during interrogation. ● Polygraph results are inadmissible as evidence in most states.—Also termed *lie detector*.

positive law. A system of law implemented and laid down within a particular political community by political superiors, as distinct from moral law, natural law, or law existing in an ideal community or in some nonpolitical community. ● Positive law typically consists of enacted law—the statutes and regulations that are applied and enforced in the courts. Cf. NATURAL LAW.

possession. **1.** The fact of having or holding property in one's power; the exercise of dominion over property. **2.** The right under which one may exercise control over something to the exclusion of all others; the continuing exercise of a claim to the exclusive use of a material object. **3.** (*usu. pl.*) Something that a person owns or controls; property.

power of attorney. **1.** An instrument granting someone authority to act as agent or attorney-in-fact for the grantor. **2.** The authority so granted.

prayer for relief. A request addressed to the court and appearing at the end of a pleading; esp., a request for specific relief or damages <the plaintiff's prayer for relief asked for $1 million in actual damages and $10 million in punitive damages>.

precedent (**pre**-sə-dənt), *n.* A judicial decision that serves as a basis for determining later cases involving similar facts or issues. See STARE DECISIS.

preemption. In constitutional law, the principle (derived from the Supremacy Clause) that a federal law supersedes any inconsistent state law or regulation.

preferred stock. Stock that gives its holders a preferential claim to dividends and to corporate assets upon liquidation but that usu. carries no voting rights. Cf. COMMON STOCK.

prejudice, *n.* **1.** Damage or detriment to one's legal rights or claims <the case couldn't be refiled because it had been dismissed with prejudice>. **2.** A preconceived judgment formed without a factual basis; a strong bias <the witness admitted a strong prejudice against insurance companies>.

preliminary hearing. A criminal hearing (usu. conducted by a magistrate) to determine whether there is sufficient evidence to prosecute an accused person. ● If sufficient evidence exists, the case will be bound over for grand-jury review or an information will be filed in the trial court.

premeditation. Conscious consideration and planning that precedes some act (esp. the commission of a crime).

premises liability. A landowner's or landholder's tort liability for conditions or activities on the premises.

prenuptial agreement. An agreement made before marriage usu. to resolve issues of support and property division if the marriage ends in divorce or by the death of a spouse.

preponderance of the evidence. The greater weight of the evidence; the burden of proof in a civil trial, in which the jury is instructed to find for the party that, on the whole, has the stronger evidence, however slight the edge may be.

prescription. The acquisition of an interest (esp. an easement) in real property—but not full title—by open and continuous possession over a statutory period. Cf. ADVERSE POSSESSION.

presumption. A factual or legal assumption drawn from the existence of another fact or group of facts; a rule of evidence that calls for a certain result in a given case unless the adversely affected party overcomes it with other evidence. ● A presumption shifts the burden of production to the opposing party, who can then attempt to rebut the presumption.

presumption of innocence. The fundamental criminal-law principle that a person may not be convicted of a crime unless the prosecution proves guilt beyond a reasonable doubt, without any burden placed on the accused to prove innocence.

pretrial conference. An informal meeting at which opposing attorneys confer, sometimes with the judge, to work toward the disposition of the case by discussing matters of evidence and narrowing the issues that will be argued.

pretrial order. An order reciting a case's procedural rules, deadlines, and stipulations as agreed to by the parties usu. at a pretrial conference.

prima facie (**prı**-mə-**fay**-shə *or* -shee). [Latin "at first sight"] **1.** *adv.* On first appearance, but subject to further evidence or information <the deed is prima facie valid>. **2.** *adj.* Sufficient to establish a fact or raise a presumption unless disproved or rebutted <because the plaintiff made out a prima facie case, the judge submitted the issues to the jury>.

principal, *n.* **1.** One who authorizes another to act on his or her behalf as an agent. Cf. AGENT. **2.** One who commits or participates in a crime. Cf. ACCESSORY. **3.** One who has primary responsibility on an obligation, as opposed to a surety or indorser. **4.** The corpus of an estate or trust. **5.** The amount of a debt, investment, or other fund, not including interest or profits.

prior restraint. A governmental restriction on a publication before it is published. • Prior restraints violate the First Amendment unless the publication is legally obscene or defamatory, or unless it creates a clear and present danger to society.

privilege. **1.** A special legal right, exemption, or immunity granted to a person or class of persons <only licensed attorneys have the privilege to practice law>. **2.** An affirmative defense by which a defendant acknowledges at least part of the conduct complained of but asserts that the defendant's conduct was authorized or sanctioned by law; esp., in tort law, a circumstance justifying or excusing an intentional tort <the employer had a qualified privilege to circulate the employee's performance evaluation to her supervisors>. Cf. IMMUNITY (2). **3.** In the law of evidence, the right to prevent disclosure of certain information in court, esp. when the information was originally communicated in a professional or confidential relationship <the attorney-client privilege has several exceptions>.

privity (**pri**-vi-tee). The relationship between two contracting parties, each having a legally recognized interest in the subject matter of the contract; mutuality of interest <the buyer and seller are in privity>.—Also termed *privity of contract*.

probable cause. A reasonable ground to suspect that a person has committed a particular crime or that a place contains specific items connected with a crime. ● Under the Fourth Amendment, probable cause—which amounts to more than a bare suspicion but less than legal evidence—must be shown before an arrest warrant or search warrant may be issued.

probate (**proh**-bayt), *n.* The judicial procedure by which a testamentary document is established to be a valid will; the proving of a will to the satisfaction of the court.

probate court. A court with the power to declare wills valid or invalid, to oversee the administration of estates, and in some states to appoint guardians and approve the adoption of minors.

probation. A court-imposed criminal sentence that, subject to stated conditions, releases a convicted person into the community instead of sending the person to prison.

probative (**proh**-bə-tiv), *adj.* Tending to prove or disprove <the evidence's probative value>.

pro bono (proh-**boh**-noh), *adj.* [Latin *pro bono publico* "for the public good"] Of or relating to uncompensated legal services performed for the public good <lawyers are encouraged to handle pro bono cases>.

procedural law. The rules that prescribe the steps for having a right or duty judicially enforced, as opposed to the substantive law that defines the specific rights or duties themselves. Cf. SUBSTANTIVE LAW.

proceeding. 1. The regular and orderly progression of a lawsuit, including all acts and events between the time of commencement and the entry of judgment. **2.** Any procedural means for seeking redress from a tribunal or agency. **3.** The business conducted by a court or other official body; a hearing.

process, *n.* **1.** The proceedings in any action or prosecution <due process of law>. **2.** The summons or writ by which a person is cited to appear in court <service of process>.

products liability. 1. A manufacturer's or seller's tort liability for any damages or injuries suffered by a buyer, user, or bystander as a result of a defective product. ● Products liability can be based on theories of negligence, strict liability, or breach of warranty. **2.** The legal theory by which liability is imposed on the manufacturer or seller of a defective product; the field of law dealing with this theory.

professional corporation. A business organization formed by one or more licensed practitioners (such as lawyers or doctors) who render professional services to the public. ● A professional corporation usu. provides some level of limited liability and tax advantages to its shareholders.—Abbr. P.C.—Also termed *professional association*.

proffer (**pro**-fər), *vb.* To offer or tender (something, esp. evidence) for immediate acceptance <the defendant proffered 30 exhibits during trial>.

171

promise, *n.* **1.** The manifestation of an intention to act or refrain from acting in a specified way, so made as to justify another in understanding that a commitment has been made; a person's assurance that the person will or will not do something. ● A binding promise—one that the law will enforce—is the essence of a contract. **2.** The words in a promissory note expressing the maker's intention to pay a debt. ● A mere written acknowledgment that a debt is due is insufficient to constitute a promise.

promissory estoppel. The principle that a promise made without consideration becomes binding if (1) the promisor intends, or should reasonably expect, the promise to induce reliance, (2) a party actually relies on the promise, and (3) nonenforcement of the promise will cause injury or injustice. See ESTOPPEL.

promissory note. See NOTE.

proof. 1. The establishment or denial of an alleged fact by evidence; the persuasive effect of evidence in the mind of a fact-finder <the prosecution has the burden of proof>. **2.** Evidence that determines the finding or judgment of a court <the fingerprints and hair samples served as proof of the defendant's guilt>.

172

property. 1. The right to possess, use, and enjoy a determinate thing (either a tract of land or a chattel); the right of ownership <private property is fundamental to a free society>. 2. Any external thing over which the rights of possession, use, and enjoyment are exercised <the streets are city property>.

pro se (proh-**say**). [Latin] 1. *adj. or adv.* For oneself; on one's own behalf <the defendant didn't like his court-appointed lawyer, so he proceeded pro se at trial>. 2. *n.* A person who represents himself or herself in a court proceeding without the help of a lawyer <the pro se took three depositions in her lawsuit>.

prosecution. 1. A criminal proceeding in which an accused person is tried <the district attorney almost always seeks the death penalty in multiple-murder prosecutions>. 2. The government attorneys who initiate and maintain a criminal action against an accused defendant <the prosecution didn't know if the defendant would take the stand>. 3. The institution and carrying on of a civil action <prosecution of a civil-rights lawsuit against the police department>.

prosecutor. A lawyer who represents the government in criminal proceedings.

protection order. See RESTRAINING ORDER (1).

protective order. 1. A court order prohibiting or restricting a party from engaging in a legal procedure (esp. discovery) that unduly annoys or burdens the opposing party or a third-party witness. **2.** See RESTRAINING ORDER (1).

protest, *n*. A formal statement, usu. in writing, disputing a debt's legality or validity but agreeing to make payment while reserving the right to recover the amount at a later time <the credit purchaser paid the debt under protest>.

prove up, *vb*. To present or complete the proof of (something); to show that one has fulfilled the legal requirements <at trial, the plaintiff used affidavits to prove up his medical expenses>.

proximate cause. 1. A cause that directly produces an event and without which the event would not have occurred. **2.** A cause that is legally sufficient to result in liability.

public defender. A lawyer or staff of lawyers, usu. publicly appointed, whose duty is to represent indigent criminal defendants.— Abbr. P.D.

public figure. A person who has achieved fame or notoriety or who has voluntarily become involved in a public controversy. • A public figure suing for defamation must prove that the defendant acted with actual malice.

public law. 1. The body of law dealing with the relations between private individuals and the government, and with the operation of the government itself; constitutional law, criminal law, and administrative law taken together. **2.** A statute affecting the general public.

punitive damages. A monetary amount awarded in addition to actual damages when the defendant acted with recklessness, malice, or deceit. • Punitive damages, which are intended to punish and thus deter blameworthy conduct, are generally not recoverable for breach of contract.—Also termed *exemplary damages*.

purchase, *n.* **1.** The acquisition of property or an interest in property for money or other valuable consideration. **2.** The acquisition of real property by means other than descent or inheritance.

purchase-money security interest. A security interest that is either (1) taken or retained by the seller of the collateral to secure all or part of its price, or (2) taken by a person who by making advances or incurring an obligation gives value to enable the debtor to acquire rights in or the use of collateral if that value is in fact so used. ● If a bank loans a buyer the money to purchase a car and agrees to take an interest in the car as collateral for the loan, the bank's interest in the car is a purchase-money security interest—Abbr. PMSI.

Q

quantum meruit (**kwahn**-təm-**mer**-ə-wit).
[Latin "as much as he or she has deserved"] **1.**
The reasonable value of services; damages
awarded in an amount considered reasonable
to compensate a person who has rendered services in a quasi-contractual relationship. **2.** A
claim or cause of action for the reasonable
value of services rendered. See QUASI-CONTRACT.

quash, *vb.* To annul or make void; to terminate <quash a subpoena>.

quasi-contract. An obligation imposed by law
because of the conduct of the parties, because
of some special relationship between them, or
because one of them would otherwise be unjustly enriched. ● A quasi-contract is not actually a contract, but a remedy that allows the
plaintiff to sue to recover a benefit conferred
on the defendant.—Also termed *implied-in-law
contract*. See UNJUST ENRICHMENT.

question of fact. An issue concerning the
occurrence of actual or alleged events or circumstances, to be decided by the jury (or by
the judge in a bench trial) <the question of
fact was whether the traffic signal was red or
green>.

question of law. An issue concerning the application or interpretation of law, to be decided by the judge rather than the jury <the question of law was whether the contract with the minor was valid>.

quid pro quo (**kwid**-proh-**kwoh**). [Latin "something for something"] A thing that is exchanged for another thing of more or less equal value; a substitute <the discount was given as a quid pro quo for the extra business>. Cf. CONSIDERATION.

quiet enjoyment. The use and possession of real property free from interference or dispossession by someone with superior title <the deed contained a covenant of quiet enjoyment>.

quitclaim deed. A deed that conveys a grantor's complete interest or claim in real property but that neither warrants nor professes that the title is valid. Cf. WARRANTY DEED.

quo warranto (kwoh-**wor**-ən-toh *or* -wə-**rahn**-toh). [Law Latin "by what authority"] **1.** A common-law writ used to inquire into the authority by which a public office is held or a franchise is claimed. **2.** An action by which the state seeks to revoke a corporation's charter.

R

racketeering. 1. A system of organized crime traditionally involving the extortion of money from businesses by intimidation, violence, or other illegal methods <the gang has a well-known history of racketeering>. **2.** The practice of engaging in a fraudulent scheme or enterprise <the federal government fights racketeering with the RICO statute>.

rape, *n.* **1.** The common-law felony of having sexual intercourse with a woman without her consent, usu. by force or threat of force. **2.** Under modern statutes, unlawful sexual intercourse with a person without his or her consent. Cf. SEXUAL ASSAULT.

ratification. 1. Confirmation and acceptance of a previous act, thus making the act valid from the moment it was done <the Senate's ratification of the treaty>. **2.** In contract law, a person's binding adoption of an act already completed but either not done in a way that originally produced a legal obligation or done by a stranger having at the time no authority to act as the person's agent <an adult's ratification of a contract signed during childhood>.

ratio decidendi (**ray**-shee-oh-des-i-**den**-dee *or* **ray**-shoh-). [Latin "the reason for deciding"] The principle or rule of law on which a court's decision is founded <the majority opinion's *ratio decidendi* was in the final paragraph>.

real party in interest. A person entitled under the substantive law to enforce the right sued upon and who generally, but not necessarily, benefits from the action's final outcome.

real property. Land and anything growing on, attached to, or erected on it, excluding anything that may be severed without injury to the land. ● Real property can be either tangible (soil and buildings) or intangible (easements).—Also termed *realty*; *real estate*. Cf. PERSONAL PROPERTY.

reasonable care. As a test of liability for negligence, the degree of care that an ordinarily prudent and competent person engaged in the same conduct or endeavor should exercise under similar circumstances. See REASONABLE PERSON.

reasonable doubt. The doubt that prevents one from being firmly convinced of a defendant's guilt, or the belief that there is a real possibility that a defendant is not guilty. ● "Beyond a reasonable doubt" is the standard used by a jury to determine whether a criminal defendant is guilty, based on the presumption of innocence.

reasonable person. A hypothetical person used as a legal standard, esp. to determine whether someone acted negligently. ● The reasonable person acts sensibly, does things without serious delay, and takes proper but not excessive precautions.

reasonable suspicion. A particularized and objective basis, supported by specific and articulable facts, for suspecting a person of criminal activity. ● A police officer must have reasonable suspicion to stop a person in a public place. See STOP AND FRISK. Cf. PROBABLE CAUSE.

rebuttable presumption. An inference drawn from certain facts that establish a prima facie case, which may be overcome by the introduction of contrary evidence. Cf. CONCLUSIVE PRESUMPTION.

rebuttal. 1. In-court contradiction of an adverse party's evidence <the doctor's testimony was a rebuttal of the plaintiff's claimed injuries>. **2.** The time given to a party to present contradictory evidence or arguments <after the defense presented its case-in-chief, the prosecution began its rebuttal>.

receiver. A disinterested person appointed by a court, or by a corporation or other person, for the protection or collection of property that is the subject of diverse claims (for example, because it belongs to a bankrupt or is otherwise being litigated).

recital. **1.** An account or description of some fact or thing <the defendant disputed the plaintiff's recital of the accident>. **2.** A preliminary statement in a contract or deed explaining the background of the transaction or showing the existence of particular facts <the recitals in the lease described the parties' intentions>.

recklessness. **1.** Conduct by which the actor does not desire harmful consequence but nonetheless foresees the possibility and consciously takes the risk. ● Recklessness involves a greater degree of fault than negligence but a lesser degree of fault than intentional wrongdoing. **2.** The state of mind in which a person does not care about the consequences of his or her actions.

record, *n.* **1.** A written account of past events, usu. designed to memorialize those events. **2.** The official report of the proceedings in a case, including the filed papers, a verbatim transcript, and tangible exhibits.

recourse (**ree**-kors). In commercial law, the right of a holder of a negotiable instrument to demand repayment from the drawer or indorser if the instrument is dishonored.

recusal (ri-**kyoo**-zəl). The removal or disqualification of a judge in a particular case, esp. because of a conflict of interest.

redemption. **1.** The act or an instance of reclaiming or regaining possession by paying a specific price; esp., the payment of a defaulted mortgage debt by a borrower who does not want to lose the property. **2.** In bankruptcy, a debtor's right to repurchase property from a buyer who obtained the property at a forced sale initiated by a creditor. **3.** In corporate law, the reacquisition of a security by the issuer. • Redemption usu. refers to the repurchase of a bond before maturity, but it may also refer to the repurchase of stock and mutual-fund shares.

redlining. Unlawful refusal by financial institutions or insurance companies to make loans or issue policies to people living in allegedly bad neighborhoods.

reformation. An equitable remedy by which a court will modify a written agreement to reflect the actual intent of the parties, usu. to correct fraud or mutual mistake, such as an incomplete property description in a deed.

regulation. 1. The act or process of controlling by rule or restriction <state regulation of insurance companies>. **2.** A rule or order, having legal force, issued by an administrative agency or a local government <various OSHA regulations>.

rehabilitation. 1. In criminal law, the improvement of a criminal's character so that he or she can function in society without committing crimes in the future <many believe that rehabilitation of hardened criminals cannot be achieved>. **2.** In evidence, the restoration of a witness's credibility after the witness has been impeached on cross-examination <the inconsistencies were explained away during the plaintiff's rehabilitation of the witness>. **3.** In bankruptcy law, the process of reorganizing a debtor's financial affairs so that the debtor may continue to exist as a financial entity and creditors may satisfy their claims from the debtor's future earnings <the corporation's rehabilitation was successful>.

rehearing. A second or subsequent hearing of a case or an appeal, usu. held to review an alleged error in the first hearing <the appel-

lant filed a motion for rehearing after the court rejected the appeal>.

relator. **1.** The real party in interest in whose name a state or an attorney general brings a lawsuit. **2.** The applicant for a writ, esp. a writ of mandamus or quo warranto.

release, *n.* **1.** Liberation from an obligation, duty, or demand; the act of giving up a right or claim to the person against whom it could have been enforced <the employee asked for a release from his contract so he could take another job>. **2.** A written discharge, acquittance, or receipt <the settlement agreement included a release from future liability>.

relevant, *adj.* Tending to prove or disprove a fact that is of consequence in a case <relevant evidence>.

relief. See REMEDY.

remainder. A future interest arising in a third person—that is, someone other than the creator of the estate or the creator's heirs—who is intended to take after the natural termination of the preceding estate. ● For example, if a grant is "to A for life, and then to B," B's future interest is a remainder.

remand (ri-**mand**), *vb*. **1.** To send (a case) back to the court from which it came for some further action <the appellate court reversed the trial court's judgment and remanded the case for a new trial>. **2.** To recommit (an accused) to custody after a preliminary examination <after the hearing, the trial court remanded the defendant into custody>.

remedy, *n*. The enforcement of a right or the redress of an injury, esp. by monetary damages.—Also termed *relief*.

removal. 1. The transfer or moving of a person or thing from one location, position, or residence to another <the merchant's removal of the goods to another state violated the security agreement>. **2.** The transfer of an action from one court to another, esp. from a state court to a federal court <the plaintiff challenged the defendant's removal of the case to federal court from state court>.

render, *vb*. **1.** To issue or announce formally <the jury rendered its verdict>. **2.** To deliver or perform <the buyer rendered payment>.

rendition. 1. The action of making, delivering, or giving out something, such as a legal decision. **2.** The return of a fugitive from one state to the state where the fugitive is accused or convicted of a crime. See EXTRADITION.

renunciation (ri-nən[t]-see-**ay**-shən). **1.** The express or tacit abandonment of a right without transferring it to another. **2.** In criminal law, complete and voluntary abandonment of criminal purpose—sometimes coupled with an attempt to thwart the activity's success—before a crime is committed. ● Renunciation can be an affirmative defense to attempt, conspiracy, and the like. **3.** In wills and estates, the act of waiving a right under a will and claiming instead a statutory share.

reorganization. In bankruptcy law, a financial restructuring of a corporation, esp. in the repayment of debts, under a plan created by a trustee and approved by a court. See CHAPTER 11.

reply, *n.* A plaintiff's response to a defendant's allegation or counterclaim.

representation. 1. A presentation of fact—either by words or by conduct—made to induce someone to act, esp. to enter into a contract <Grace bought the car because of the seller's representation that it had never been in an accident>. Cf. MISREPRESENTATION. **2.** The act or an instance of standing for or acting on behalf of another, esp. by a lawyer on behalf of a client <the defendant was dissatisfied with his court-appointed attorney's representation>. **3.** The assumption by an heir of the rights and obligations of his or her predecessor <each child takes a share by representation>. See PER STIRPES.

repudiation (ri-pyoo-dee-**ay**-shən). The rejection or refusal of a duty or obligation (esp. a contractual one). See ANTICIPATORY REPUDIATION.

request for admission. In pretrial discovery, a party's written factual statements served on another party who must admit, deny, or object to the substance of each statement. ● The admissions will be treated by the court as established, and therefore do not have to be proved at trial.

request for production. In pretrial discovery, a party's written request that another party present specified documents or other tangible things for inspection and copying by the requesting party.

res (rays *or* reez *or* rez). [Latin "thing"] **1.** An object, interest, or status, as opposed to a person <jurisdiction of the res—the real property in Colorado>. **2.** A trust corpus <the stock certificate is the res of the trust>.

188

rescission (ri-**sizh**-ən). **1.** A party's unilateral unmaking of a contract for a legally sufficient reason, such as the other party's material breach. ● Rescission is generally available as a remedy or defense for the nonbreaching party and restores the parties to their precontractual positions. **2.** An agreement by contracting parties to discharge all remaining duties of performance and terminate the contract.

res gestae (rays-**jes**-tı *or* -tay *or* -tee). [Latin "things done"] The events at issue, or other events contemporaneous with them. ● In the law of evidence, words and statements about the res gestae are usu. admissible under a hearsay exception.

res ipsa loquitur (rays-ip-sə-**loh**-kwə-tər). [Latin "the thing speaks for itself"] **1.** In tort law, the doctrine that, in some circumstances, the mere fact of an accident's occurrence raises an inference of negligence sufficient to establish a prima facie case. **2.** In criminal law, a test used to determine whether a defendant has gone beyond preparation and committed an attempt, based on whether the defendant's act itself indicated to an observer what the defendant intended to do.

res judicata (rays-joo-di-**kah**-tə *or* -**kay**-tə). [Latin "a thing adjudicated"] **1.** An issue that

has been definitively settled by judicial decision. **2.** An affirmative defense barring the
same parties from litigating a second lawsuit
on the same claim. ● The three essential elements are (1) an earlier decision on the identical issue, (2) a final judgment on the merits,
and (3) the involvement of the same parties or
parties in privity with the original parties. Cf.
COLLATERAL ESTOPPEL.

respondeat superior (ri-**spon**-dee-aht-soo-
pir-ee-or). [Latin "let the master respond"]
The common-law doctrine holding an employer
or principal liable for the employee's or agent's
actions (including torts) committed during the
scope of employment. See VICARIOUS LIABILITY.

respondent. 1. The party against whom an
appeal is taken; an appellee. **2.** The party
against whom a motion or petition is filed. Cf.
PETITIONER.

rest, *vb.* (Of a litigant) to voluntarily conclude
presenting evidence in a trial <after the police
officer's testimony, the prosecution rested>.

restitution. 1. The return or restoration of
some specific thing to its rightful owner or
status. **2.** Compensation for benefits derived
from a wrong done to another. **3.** Compensation or reparation for the loss caused to an-

other. ● Restitution is available in tort and contract law and is sometimes ordered as a condition of probation in criminal law.

restraining order. 1. A court order prohibiting or restricting a person from harassing, threatening, and sometimes even contacting or approaching another specified person. ● This type of restraining order is issued most commonly in cases of domestic violence.—Also termed *protection order*; *protective order*. **2.** See TEMPORARY RESTRAINING ORDER.

restraint of trade. An agreement between or combination of businesses intended to eliminate competition, create a monopoly, artificially raise prices, or otherwise adversely affect the free market. ● Restraints of trade are usu. illegal, but may be declared reasonable if they are in the best interests of both the parties and the public.

restrictive covenant. 1. A private agreement, usu. in a deed or lease, that restricts the use and occupancy of real property, esp. by specifying lot size, building lines, architectural styles, and the uses to which the property may be put. **2.** A noncompetition clause.

resulting trust. A trust imposed by law when someone transfers property under circumstances suggesting that he or she did not intend the transferee to have the beneficial interest in the property. Cf. CONSTRUCTIVE TRUST.

retainer. 1. A client's authorization for a lawyer to act in a case <the lawyer needed an express retainer before making a settlement offer>. **2.** A fee paid to a lawyer to secure legal representation <the firm's usual retainer for murder cases is $20,000>.

reverse, *vb.* To set aside or nullify (a lower court's decision) <the court of appeals reversed the trial court's judgment>. Cf. AFFIRM (1).

reversion. A future interest in land arising by operation of law whenever an estate owner grants to another a particular estate, such as a life estate or a term of years, but does not dispose of the entire interest. ● A reversion occurs automatically upon termination of the prior estate, as when a life tenant dies.

revocation (rev-ə-**kay**-shən). **1.** An annulment, cancellation, or reversal, usu. of an act or power. **2.** In contract law, withdrawal of an offer by the offeror. **3.** In wills and estates, invalidation of a will by the testator, either by destroying the will or executing a new one.

right, *n.* An interest or expectation guaranteed by law; a legally recognized and protected interest the violation of which is a wrong.

right of privacy. 1. The right to personal autonomy. ● The U.S. Constitution does not explicitly provide for a right of privacy, but the Supreme Court has repeatedly ruled that this right is implied in the "zones of privacy" created by other constitutional guarantees. **2.** The right of a person and his or her property to be free from unwarranted public scrutiny or exposure. See INVASION OF PRIVACY.

right of survivorship. The right of a property owner who survives a coowner's death to take the coowner's share and own the property in full. ● The right of survivorship exists in a joint tenancy but not in a tenancy in common.

right of way. 1. The right, established by usage or by contract, to pass through grounds or property owned by another. See EASEMENT. **2.** The right to take precedence in traffic.

robbery. The illegal taking of property from the person of another, or in the person's presence, by violence or intimidation. Cf. BURGLARY.

royalty. 1. A payment made to an author or inventor for each copy of a work or article sold under a copyright or patent. **2.** A share of the product or profit from real property, reserved by the grantor of a mineral lease, in exchange for the lessee's right to mine or drill on the land.

rule, *n.* **1.** An established and authoritative standard or principle <a rule of law>. **2.** A regulation governing a court's or an agency's internal procedures <rules of criminal procedure>.

rule against perpetuities. In property law, the rule prohibiting a grant of an estate unless the interest must vest, if at all, no later than 21 years after the death of some person alive when the interest is created.

rulemaking. The process used by an administrative agency to formulate, amend, or appeal a rule or regulation.

S

sale. The transfer of property for a price; the agreement by which such a transfer takes place.

sanction, *n.* **1.** A recognized authority's official approval or confirmation of an action <the board of directors gave sanction to the CEO's proposal>. **2.** An enforcement mechanism • used to ensure compliance with the law, international agreements, or court rules and orders by either imposing a penalty for violations or offering a reward for observances; the penalty imposed or reward offered under such a mechanism <the trial court imposed sanctions on the plaintiff for discovery abuse>.

satisfaction. **1.** The giving of something with the intention, express or implied, that it is to extinguish some existing legal or moral obligation. • Satisfaction differs from performance because it is always something given as a substitute for or equivalent of something else, while performance is the identical thing promised to be done. **2.** The fulfillment of an obligation; esp., the payment in full of a debt.

scienter (see-**en**-tər *or* sı-). [Latin "knowingly"] **1.** The fact of an act's having been done knowingly, esp. as a ground for damages or criminal punishment. **2.** Prior knowledge or intention. **3.** Loosely, guilty knowledge; *mens rea.*

search, *n.* An inspection of a person's body, property, or other area that the person would reasonably be expected to consider as private, conducted by a law-enforcement officer for the purpose of finding evidence of a crime. ● Because the Fourth Amendment prohibits unreasonable searches (as well as seizures), a search cannot ordinarily be conducted without probable cause.

search warrant. A judge's written order, on behalf of the state, authorizing a law-enforcement officer to search for and seize evidence at a specified location. Cf. ARREST WARRANT.

Second Amendment. The constitutional amendment, ratified with the Bill of Rights in 1791, guaranteeing the right to keep and bear arms. ● The Supreme Court has narrowly defined this right so as not to prevent the state and federal governments from enacting gun-control legislation.

secured transaction. A business arrangement by which a buyer or borrower gives collateral to the seller or lender to guarantee payment of an obligation.

security. 1. Collateral given or pledged to guarantee the fulfillment of an obligation <security for a loan>. **2.** An instrument that evidences the holder's ownership rights in a firm (such as a stock), the holder's creditor relationship with a firm or government (such as a bond), or the holder's other ownership rights (such as an option) <a diverse portfolio of securities>.

security agreement. An agreement that creates or provides for a security interest in specified real or personal property to guarantee the performance of an obligation.

security interest. A property interest created by agreement or by operation of law to secure performance of an obligation (esp. repayment of a debt). • In most contexts, a security interest is in personal property (as opposed to a mortgage, which is ordinarily an interest in real property).

self-dealing. The act or an instance of a fiduciary's using another's property for his or her own benefit.

self-defense. The use of force to protect oneself from a real or threatened attack. • Generally, a person is justified in using a reasonable amount of force in self-defense if he or she believes that bodily harm is imminent and that force is necessary to avoid this harm. In many states, the justification is extended to include the defense of other persons or of one's property.

self-incrimination. An act or declaration by which a party explicitly or implicitly admits a personal involvement with a crime. • Under the Fifth Amendment, a person has a constitutional privilege against self-incrimination.

sentence. The judgment that a court formally pronounces after finding a criminal defendant guilty; the punishment imposed on a criminal wrongdoer <although Biggs received a life sentence, he will be eligible for parole in 30 years>.

separate property. Property that a spouse owned before marriage or acquired during marriage through an inheritance or by gift from a third party, or property acquired during marriage but after the spouses have entered into a separation agreement and begun living apart. Cf. COMMUNITY PROPERTY.

sequestration (see-kwes-**tray**-shən). **1.** The process by which property is removed from its possessor pending the outcome of a dispute in which two or more parties contend for it. Cf.

ATTACHMENT; GARNISHMENT. **2.** Custodial isolation of a jury to prevent tampering and exposure to publicity, or of witnesses to prevent them from hearing the testimony of others.

service. 1. The formal delivery of a writ, summons, or other legal process <after several attempts, service still had not been accomplished by the constable>.—Also termed *service of process*. **2.** The formal delivery of some other legal notice, such as a pleading <a certificate of service is attached to the motion>.

setoff. 1. A defendant's counterdemand against the plaintiff, arising out of a transaction independent of the plaintiff's claim. **2.** A debtor's right to reduce the amount of a debt by any sum the creditor owes the debtor; the counterbalancing sum owed by the creditor.

setting. The date and time established by a court for a trial or hearing <the plaintiff asked the judge for a December trial setting>.

settlement. 1. An agreement to end a dispute or lawsuit <the parties reached a settlement the day before trial>. **2.** A real-estate closing <the settlement on their first home is next Monday>. **3.** The closing of a decedent's estate by the executor <the settlement of the tycoon's estate was long and complex>.

settlor. A person who establishes a trust for the benefit of another.—Also termed *donor*; *grantor*.

sever, *vb.* To separate (a claim or party) into distinct actions to avoid prejudice against a party or for judicial convenience <the court severed the bad-faith claim from the breach-of-contract suit>.

sexual assault. The intentional touching of another person in a sexual way without that person's consent. ● Several state statutes have abolished the crime of rape and replaced it with the offense of sexual assault.—Also termed *indecent assault*.

sexual harassment. A type of employment discrimination consisting in verbal or physical abuse of a sexual nature.

shareholder. The person in whose name stock is issued and registered by the corporation.—Also termed *stockholder*.

shareholder derivative suit. See DERIVATIVE ACTION.

shepardize, *vb.* **1.** (*often cap.*) To determine the subsequent history of (a case) by using a printed or computerized version of *Shepard's*

Citators. **2.** Loosely, to check the precedential value of (a case).

show-cause order. An order directing a party to appear in court and explain why the party took (or failed to take) some action or why the court should or should not grant some relief. ● A show-cause order is usu. issued in a contempt proceeding.

sidebar conference. 1. A discussion among the judge and counsel, usu. over an evidentiary objection, outside the jury's hearing. **2.** A discussion, esp. during voir dire, between the judge and a juror or prospective juror.—Often shortened to *sidebar*.

slander, *n*. A defamatory statement expressed in a transitory form, esp. speech. ● Unlike libel, damages from slander are not presumed and thus must be proved by the plaintiff (unless the defamation is slander per se). See DEF-AMATION. Cf. LIBEL.

slander of title. A false statement, made orally or in writing, that casts doubt on another person's ownership of property.

small-claims court. A court that informally and expeditiously adjudicates claims that seek damages below a specified monetary amount, usu. a claim to collect a small account or debt.

sobriety test. Any method of determining whether a person is intoxicated, including coordination tests and mechanical devices that measure the blood-alcohol content of a person's breath sample.

sole proprietorship. A form of business in which one person owns all the assets, owes all the liabilities, and conducts affairs in his or her own capacity, often under an assumed name.

solicitation. 1. The criminal offense of urging, advising, commanding, or otherwise inciting another to commit a crime <solicitation of murder>. ● Solicitation is a separate offense from the solicited crime. **2.** An offer to pay or accept money in exchange for sex <the prostitute was charged with solicitation>. **3.** An attempt or effort to gain business <the lawyer's solicitations took the form of radio and television ads>. ● Some states place certain prohibitions on lawyers' direct solicitation of potential clients.

sovereign immunity. 1. A government's immunity from being sued in its own courts without its consent. ● Congress has waived much of the federal government's sovereign immunity. **2.** A state's immunity from being sued in federal court by the state's own citizens.

specific intent. The intent to accomplish the precise criminal act that one is later charged with. ● At common law, the specific-intent crimes were robbery, assault, larceny, burglary, forgery, false pretenses, embezzlement, attempt, solicitation, and conspiracy.

specific performance. A court-ordered remedy that requires precise fulfillment of a legal or contractual obligation when monetary damages are inappropriate or inadequate, as when the sale of real estate or rare articles is involved. ● Specific performance is an equitable remedy that lies within the court's discretion to award whenever the common-law remedy is insufficient, either because damages would be inadequate or because the damages could not possibly be established.

speedy trial. A criminal trial that the prosecution, with reasonable diligence, begins promptly and conducts expeditiously. ● The Sixth Amendment secures the right to a speedy trial. In deciding whether an accused has been deprived of that right, courts generally consider the length of the delay, the reason for the delay, and the prejudice to the accused.

spendthrift trust. A trust that prohibits the beneficiary from assigning his or her equitable interest and also prevents a creditor from attaching that interest.

spoliation (spoh-lee-**ay**-shən). The intentional destruction, mutilation, alteration, or concealment of evidence, usu. a document. ● If proved, spoliation may be used to establish that the evidence was unfavorable to the party responsible.

spousal support. See ALIMONY.

standard of care. In the law of negligence, the degree of care that a reasonable person should exercise <the doctor's standard of care in a medical-malpractice case>.

standing. A party's right to make a legal claim or seek judicial enforcement of a duty or right <the court dismissed the case because the taxpayer did not have standing to sue>.

stare decisis (stahr-ee-də-**si**-səs *or* stair-). [Latin "to stand by things decided"] The doctrine of precedent, under which it is necessary for courts to follow earlier judicial decisions when the same points arise again in litigation. See PRECEDENT.

state action. Anything done by a government; esp., in constitutional law, an intrusion on a person's rights (esp. civil rights) either by a governmental entity or by a private requirement that can be enforced only by governmental action (such as a racially restrictive covenant, which requires judicial action for enforcement).

state court. A court of the state judicial system, as opposed to a federal court.

statement of facts. A party's presentation of the facts leading up to or surrounding a legal dispute, usu. recited toward the beginning of a brief.

state of mind. 1. The condition or capacity of a person's mind; *mens rea*. **2.** Loosely, a person's reasons or motives for committing an act, esp. a criminal act.

statute. A law enacted by a legislative body.

statute of frauds. A statute that, in order to prevent fraud and perjury, requires certain contracts to be in writing and signed by the parties. • Most statutes of frauds apply to the following types of contracts: (1) a contract of an executor or administrator to answer for a decedent's debt; (2) a contract to guarantee the debt or duty of another; (3) a contract made in consideration of marriage; (4) a contract for the sale or transfer of an interest in land; (5) a contract that cannot be performed within one year of its making; and (6) a contract for the sale of goods valued at $500 or more.

statute of limitations. A statute establishing a time limit for suing or for prosecuting a crime, based on the date when the claim accrues (usu. when the injury occurs). ● The purpose of such a statute is to require diligent prosecution of known claims, thereby providing finality and predictability in legal affairs and ensuring that claims will be resolved while evidence is reasonably available and fresh.

statutory construction. 1. The act or process of interpreting a statute. **2.** Collectively, the principles developed by courts for interpreting statutes.

statutory law. The body of law derived from statutes rather than from constitutions or judicial decisions.

statutory rape. Unlawful sexual intercourse with a person under the age of consent (as defined by statute), regardless of whether it is against that person's will.

stay, *n.* **1.** The postponement or halting of a proceeding, judgment, or the like. **2.** An order to suspend all or part of a judicial proceeding or judgment resulting from that proceeding.

stipulation. 1. A material condition or requirement in an agreement <the stipulation in the lease required payment on the first day of each month>. **2.** A voluntary agreement between opposing parties concerning some relevant point <the plaintiff and defendant entered into a stipulation on the authenticity of the exhibits>.

stock, *n.* **1.** The capital or principal fund raised by a corporation through subscribers' contributions or the sale of shares <Acme's stock is worth far more today than it was 20 years ago>. **2.** A proportional part of a corporation's capital, represented by the number of units (or shares) that one owns, and granting the holder the right to participate in the company's general management and to share in its net profits or earnings <Julia sold her IBM stock>.

stockholder. See SHAREHOLDER.

stop and frisk, *n.* A police officer's brief detention, questioning, and search of a person for a concealed weapon when the officer rea-

207

sonably suspects the person has committed or is about to commit a crime. ● The stop and frisk, which can be conducted without a warrant or probable cause, was held constitutional by the Supreme Court in *Terry v. Ohio*, 392 U.S. 1 (1968).—Also termed *investigatory stop*; *Terry stop*. See REASONABLE SUSPICION.

strict liability. Liability that does not depend on actual negligence or intent to harm, but that is based on the breach of an absolute duty to make something safe. ● Strict liability most often applies to cases involving ultrahazardous activities or products liability.

subjective standard. A legal standard that is peculiar to a particular person and based on the person's individual views and experiences. ● In criminal law, for example, premeditation is determined by a subjective standard because it depends on the defendant's mental state. Cf. OBJECTIVE STANDARD.

subject-matter jurisdiction. Jurisdiction over the nature of the case and the type of relief sought; the extent to which a court can claim to affect the conduct of persons or the status of things. Cf. PERSONAL JURISDICTION.

sublease. A lease by a lessee to a third party, conveying some or all of the leased property for a shorter term than that of the lessee, who retains a reversion in the lease.

suborn (sə-**born**), *vb.* **1.** To induce (a person) to commit an unlawful or wrongful act, esp. in a secret or underhanded manner. **2.** To induce (a person) to commit perjury. **3.** To obtain (perjured testimony) from another.

subpoena (sə-**pee**-nə). A court order commanding the appearance of a witness, subject to penalty for noncompliance.

subpoena duces tecum (doo-səs-**tee**-kəm *or* -**tay**-kəm). A subpoena ordering the witness not only to appear but also to bring specified documents.

subrogation (səb-rə-**gay**-shən). **1.** The substitution of one party for another whose debts the party pays, entitling the paying party to rights, remedies, or securities that would otherwise go to the debtor. ● For example, a surety who has paid on the principal debtor's debt is entitled to subrogation to all the securities held by the creditor and to any judgment in which the debt has been merged, and the surety may enforce those securities and rights against the debtor in any way in which the creditor might have enforced them. **2.** The principle under which an insurer that has paid the loss under an indemnity policy is entitled to take on all the rights and remedies belonging to the insured against a third party with respect to any injuries or breaches covered by the policy.

substantial-performance doctrine. The equitable rule that, if a good-faith attempt to perform does not precisely meet the terms of the agreement, the agreement will still be considered complete if the essential purpose of the contract is accomplished.

substantive law. The part of the law that creates, defines, and regulates the rights, duties, and powers of parties. Cf. PROCEDURAL LAW.

succession. The acquisition of rights or property by inheritance under the laws of descent and distribution.

sue, *vb.* To institute a lawsuit against (another party).

suit. Any proceeding brought in court against another to enforce a right or claim.

summary judgment. A judgment granted on a claim about which there is no genuine issue of material fact and upon which the movant is entitled to prevail as a matter of law. • This procedural device allows the speedy disposition of a controversy without the need for trial.

summation. See CLOSING ARGUMENT.

summons. 1. A writ or process commencing the plaintiff's action and requiring the defendant to appear and answer. **2.** A notice requiring a person to appear in court as a juror or witness.

supplemental pleading. A pleading that either corrects a defect in an earlier pleading or addresses facts arising since the earlier pleading was filed. ● Unlike an amended pleading, a supplemental pleading merely adds to the earlier pleading and does not replace it. Cf. AMENDED PLEADING.

support trust. A trust in which the trustee pays to the beneficiary only as much trust income as the trustee believes is needed for the beneficiary's support. ● As with a spendthrift trust, the beneficiary's interest cannot be assigned or reached by creditors.

suppression of evidence. 1. A trial judge's ruling that evidence that a party has offered should be excluded because it was illegally acquired. **2.** The destruction of evidence or the refusal to give evidence at a criminal proceeding. **3.** The prosecution's withholding from the defense of evidence that favors the defendant.

supra (**soo**-prə). [Latin "above"] Earlier in this text. ● *Supra* is used as a citational signal to refer to a previously cited authority. Cf. IN-FRA.

Supremacy Clause. The clause—contained in Art. VI of the U.S. Constitution—declaring that all laws made in furtherance of the Constitution and all treaties made under the authority of the United States are the "supreme law of the land" and enjoy legal superiority over any conflicting provision of a state constitution or law. See PREEMPTION.

Supreme Court. 1. The court of last resort in the federal system, whose members are appointed by the President and approved by the Senate. ● The Court was established in 1789 by Art. III, sec. 1 of the U.S. Constitution, which vests the Court with the "judicial power of the United States." **2.** An appellate court existing in most states, usu. as the court of last resort. **3.** In New York, a court of general jurisdiction with trial and appellate divisions. ● The Court of Appeals is the court of last resort in New York.

surety (**shuur**[-ə]-tee). **1.** A person who is primarily liable for the payment of another's debt or the performance of another's obligation. ● Although a surety is similar to an insurer, one important difference is that a surety often receives no compensation for assuming liability. **2.** A formal assurance; esp., a pledge, bond, guarantee, or security given for the fulfillment of an undertaking.

survival action. A lawsuit brought on behalf of a decedent's estate for injuries or damages incurred by the decedent immediately before death. Cf. WRONGFUL-DEATH ACTION.

survivorship. See RIGHT OF SURVIVORSHIP.

sustain, *vb.* (Of a court) to uphold or rule in favor of <the objection was sustained>.

symbolic speech. Conduct that expresses an opinion or conveys a message, such as a hunger strike or the wearing of an armband. ● As with purely oral or written expression, symbolic speech is generally protected under the First Amendment.

T

tax, *n.* A monetary charge imposed by the government on persons, entities, or property to yield public revenue. ● The term embraces all the regular impositions made by government on the person, property, privileges, occupations, and enjoyment of the people, and includes duties, imposts, and excises.

temporary restraining order. A court order preserving the status quo until the plaintiff's application for a preliminary or permanent injunction can be heard. ● A temporary restraining order may be granted without notifying the defendant in advance.—Abbr. TRO.— Often shortened to *restraining order*. Cf. IN- JUNCTION.

tenancy. 1. The possession or occupancy of land by right or title, esp. under a lease; a leasehold interest in real estate. **2.** The period of such possession or occupancy.

tenancy in common. A tenancy by two or more persons, in equal or unequal undivided shares, each person having an equal right to possess the whole property but no right of survivorship. Cf. JOINT TENANCY.

tenant. 1. One who holds or possesses real property by any kind of right or title. **2.** One who pays rent for the temporary use and occupation of another's real property under a lease or similar arrangement.

tender, *n*. **1.** An unconditional offer of money or performance to satisfy a debt or obligation <a tender of delivery>. ● The tender may save the tendering party from a penalty for nonpayment or nonperformance or may, if the other party unjustifiably refuses the tender, place the other party in default. **2.** An offer or bid put forward for acceptance <a tender for the construction contract>. **3.** Something that serves as a means of payment, such as coin, bank notes, or other circulating medium; money <legal tender>.

***Terry* stop.** See STOP AND FRISK.

testacy (**tes**-tə-see). The fact or condition of leaving a valid will at one's death. Cf. INTESTA-CY.

testament. A will that disposes of personal property.

testamentary, *adj*. **1.** Of or relating to a will or testament <testamentary intent>. **2.** Provided for or appointed by a will <testamentary guardian>. **3.** Created by a will <testamentary gift>.

testamentary capacity. The mental condition a person must have when making a will in order for the will to be considered valid. • This capacity is often described as the ability to recognize one's heirs and the nature and extent of one's estate.

testate, *adj.* Having made or left a valid will <he died testate>.

testator (**tes**-tay-tər). A person who has made a will; esp., a person who dies leaving a will.

testify, *vb.* To give evidence under oath or affirmation as a witness <the witness was sworn in before she began testifying>.

testimony. Evidence that a witness under oath or affirmation gives at trial or in an affidavit or deposition.

theft. 1. The felonious taking and removing of another's personal property with the intent of depriving the true owner of it; larceny. **2.** Broadly, any act or instance of stealing, including larceny, burglary, embezzlement, and false pretenses. • Many modern penal codes have consolidated these property offenses under the name "theft."

third party. One who is not a party to a lawsuit, agreement, or other transaction but who is somehow involved in the transaction; someone other than the principal parties.

third-party beneficiary. A person who is not a party to a contract but who stands to benefit from the contract's performance. ● For example, if Alice and Bill agree to a contract under which Bill will render some performance to Charles, then Charles is a third-party beneficiary.

title. 1. The union of all elements (as ownership, possession, and custody) constituting the legal right to control and dispose of property; the legal link between a person who owns property and the property itself <after paying off the mortgage, Lisa had title to the house>. **2.** Legal evidence of a person's ownership rights in property; an instrument (such as a deed) that constitutes such evidence <George kept his car's title in the glove compartment>. **3.** The heading of a legal document or proceeding <the title of the contract was "Confidentiality Agreement">. **4.** A subdivision of a statute or code <Title VII governs employment discrimination>.

title search. An examination of the public records to determine whether any defects or encumbrances exist in a given property's chain of title. ● Title searches are typically conducted by title companies or real-estate lawyers at a prospective buyer's or mortgagee's request.

tort. 1. A civil wrong for which a remedy may be obtained, usu. in the form of damages; a breach of a duty that the law imposes on everyone. **2.** (*pl.*) The branch of law dealing with such wrongs.

tortfeasor. One who commits a tort; a wrongdoer.

tortious (**tor**-shəs), *adj.* **1.** Constituting a tort; wrongful <tortious conduct>. **2.** In the nature of a tort <tortious cause of action>.

tortious interference with contractual relations. A third party's intentional inducement for a contracting party to break a contract, thereby damaging the relationship between the contracting parties.

toxic tort. A tort caused by exposure to a toxic substance, such as asbestos, radiation, or hazardous waste. ● Toxic torts can be remedied by civil lawsuits (esp. class actions) or by administrative-agency actions.

trademark. A word, phrase, logo, or other graphic symbol used by a manufacturer or seller to distinguish its products from those of others. ● To receive federal protection, a trademark must be (1) distinctive rather than merely descriptive, (2) affixed to a product that is actually sold in the marketplace, and (3) registered with the U.S. Patent and Trademark Office.—Often shortened to *mark*.

tradename. A name, style, or symbol used to distinguish a company, partnership, or business (as opposed to a product or service); the name under which a business operates.

trade secret. A formula, process, device, or other business information that is kept confidential in order to maintain an advantage over competitors.

transcript. A handwritten, printed, or typed copy; esp., the official copy of the record of proceedings in a trial or hearing, as taken down by the court reporter.

transfer of venue. See CHANGE OF VENUE.

trespass, *n.* An unlawful act committed against the person or property of another; esp., wrongful entry on another's real property.

trial. A formal judicial examination and determination of evidence and legal claims in an adversary proceeding.

trial court. The court of original jurisdiction where all the evidence is first received and considered.

trial de novo (di-**noh**-voh *or* dee-). A new trial on the entire case, conducted as if there had been no trial in the first instance.

trial to the bench. See BENCH TRIAL.

TRO. *abbr.* TEMPORARY RESTRAINING ORDER.

true bill, *n.* A grand jury's notation that a criminal charge should go before a petit jury for trial <after the grand jury returned a true bill, the accused was taken into custody>. Cf. NO BILL.

trust, *n.* **1.** A fiduciary relationship in which property is held by one party (the *trustee*, who has legal title) at the request of another (the *settlor*) for the benefit of a third party (the *beneficiary*, who has equitable title). ● For a trust to be valid, it must involve specific property, reflect the settlor's intent, and be created for a lawful purpose. **2.** The property so held. See FIDUCIARY RELATIONSHIP.

trustee (trəs-**tee**). One who, having legal title to property, holds it in trust for the benefit of another and owes a fiduciary duty to that beneficiary.

trust estate. See RES (2).

turpitude. See MORAL TURPITUDE.

U

UCC. *abbr.* UNIFORM COMMERCIAL CODE.

ultrahazardous activity. In tort law, an activity (such as dynamiting) for which the actor is held strictly liable because the activity (1) involves the risk of serious harm to persons or property; (2) cannot be performed without this risk, regardless of the precautions taken; and (3) does not ordinarily occur in the community. See STRICT LIABILITY.

ultra vires (əl-trə-**vir**-eez *or* -**vi**-reez), *adj. or adv.* Beyond the scope of power allowed or granted by a corporate charter or by law; unauthorized <the officer's jewelry purchases with corporate funds were ultra vires>.

unauthorized practice of law. The practice of law by a person, typically a nonlawyer, who is not a member in good standing of a recognized bar association.

unavoidable-accident doctrine. In tort law, the rule holding no party liable for an accident that was not foreseeable and that could not have been prevented by the exercise of reasonable care. ● The modern trend is for courts to ignore this doctrine and instead rely on the basic concepts of duty, negligence, and proximate cause.

unclean-hands doctrine. See CLEAN-HANDS DOCTRINE.

unconscionable (ən-**konsh**-[ə-]nə-bəl), *adj*. **1.** (Of a person) having no conscience; unscrupulous <an unconscionable used-car salesman>. **2.** (Of an act or transaction) showing no regard for conscience; affronting the sense of justice, decency, or reasonableness <the contract is void as unconscionable>.

unconstitutional, *adj*. Contrary to or in conflict with a constitution, esp. the U.S. Constitution <the Supreme Court struck down the vagrancy law as unconstitutional>.

undue influence. The improper use of power or trust in a way that deprives a person of free will and substitutes another's objective. ● Consent to a contract, transaction, or relationship is voidable if the consent is obtained through undue influence. For example, when a beneficiary unduly influences the making of a will, a probate court may invalidate that will.

unfair competition. 1. Dishonest or fraudulent rivalry in trade and commerce; esp., the practice of trying to substitute one's own goods or products in the market for those of another by means of imitating or counterfeiting the name, brand, size, shape, or other distinctive characteristic of the article or packaging. **2.** The body of law protecting the first user of such a name, brand, size, shape, or other distinctive characteristic against an imitating or counterfeiting competitor.

Uniform Commercial Code. A uniform law—adopted in some form in most states—that governs commercial transactions, including sales of goods, secured transactions, and negotiable instruments.—Abbr. UCC.

unilateral mistake. An erroneous belief by only one party to a contract. ● A unilateral mistake is usu. not grounds for rescission of the contract. Cf. MUTUAL MISTAKE.

union. A workers' organization formed to collectively negotiate with employers about such issues as salary, benefits, hours, and working conditions.—Also termed *labor union*.

United States Code Annotated. A multivolume publication of the complete text of the United States Code (the codification of federal statutory law) with historical notes, cross-references, and casenotes of federal and state decisions construing specific Code sections.—Abbr. USCA.

unjust enrichment. 1. A benefit obtained from another, not intended as a gift and not legally justifiable, for which the beneficiary must make restitution or recompense. **2.** The area of law dealing with unjustifiable benefits of this kind.

U.S. Attorney. A lawyer appointed by the President to represent, under the direction of the Attorney General, the federal government in civil and criminal cases in a federal judicial district.

USCA. *abbr.* UNITED STATES CODE ANNOTATED.

use (yoos), *n.* **1.** The application, employment, or enjoyment of something <the lot was restricted to residential use only>. **2.** A benefit or profit; esp., the right to take profits from land owned and possessed by another <a springing use arises on the occurrence of a future event>.

usury (**yoo**-zə-ree *or* **yoozh**-[ə-]ree). **1.** The crime of lending money at an illegally high rate of interest. **2.** An illegally high rate or amount of interest.

V

vacate, *vb.* **1.** To nullify or cancel <the appellate court vacated the judgment>. **2.** To physically surrender occupancy or possession of; to leave <the tenant vacated the premises>.

venire (və-**neer** *or*-**nır** *or* -**nı**-ree). A panel of persons who have been selected for jury duty and from among whom the jurors are to be chosen.—Also termed *array*; *jury panel*.

venue (**ven**-yoo). [Law French "coming"] **1.** The proper or a possible place for the trial of a lawsuit, usu. because the place has some connection with the events that have given rise to the lawsuit. **2.** The county or other territory over which a trial court has jurisdiction. Cf. JURISDICTION.

verdict. 1. A jury's finding or decision on the factual issues of a case. **2.** Loosely, in a nonjury trial, a judge's resolution of the issues of a case.

verification. 1. A formal declaration made in the presence of an authorized officer, such as a notary public, by which one swears to the truth of the statements in the document. Cf. ACKNOWLEDGMENT (1). **2.** An oath or affirmation that an authorized officer administers to an affiant or deponent.

vest, *vb.* **1.** To confer ownership of (property) upon a person. **2.** To invest (a person) with the full title to property. **3.** To give (a person) an immediate, fixed right of present or future enjoyment.

vested interest. An immediate, fixed right of present or future enjoyment.

vicarious liability. Liability that a supervisory party (such as an employer) bears for the actionable conduct of a subordinate or associate (such as an employee) because of the relationship between the two. See RESPONDEAT SUPERIOR.

void, *adj.* Of no legal effect; null <a void marriage>.

voidable, *adj.* Capable of being annulled; esp., (of a contract) capable of being affirmed or rejected at the option of one of the parties <a voidable lease>.

voir dire (vwah-**deer** *or* vor-**dir**), *n.* [Law French "to speak the truth"] **1.** A preliminary examination of a prospective juror by a judge or lawyer to decide whether the prospect is qualified and suitable to serve on a jury <during voir dire, the attorneys asked the jury panel various personal questions>. **2.** A preliminary examination to test the competence

227

of a witness or evidence <the plaintiff's attorney questioned the defendant's expert witness on voir dire>.

voluntary manslaughter. An act of murder reduced to manslaughter because of extenuating circumstances such as adequate provocation (arousing the "heat of passion") or diminished capacity. Cf. INVOLUNTARY MANSLAUGHTER.

W

waiver. 1. The voluntary relinquishment or abandonment—express or implied—of a legal right or advantage <the insurer's unconditional defense of the insured was a waiver of its claim that coverage didn't exist>. Cf. ESTOPPEL. **2.** The instrument by which a person relinquishes or abandons a legal right or advantage <Renee had to sign a waiver before the hot-air balloon ride>.

ward. A person, usu. a minor, who is under a guardian's charge or protection. See GUARDIAN.

warrant, *n.* **1.** A writ directing or authorizing someone to do an act, esp. one directing a law-enforcement officer to make an arrest, search, or seizure. **2.** A document conferring authority, esp. to pay or receive money.

warranty. 1. In contract law, an express or implied undertaking that something in furtherance of the contract is guaranteed by one of the contracting parties; esp., a seller's undertaking that the thing being sold is as represented or promised. **2.** In property law, a covenant by which the grantor in a deed binds himself or herself, as well as any heirs, to secure to the grantee the estate conveyed in the deed, and pledges to compensate the grant-

229

ee with other land if the grantee is evicted by someone having better title.

warranty deed. A deed that expressly guarantees the grantor's good, clear title and that contains covenants concerning the quality of title, including a covenant of quiet enjoyment and a defense of title against all claims. Cf. QUITCLAIM DEED.

waste, *n.* Permanent harm to real property, other than normal wear and tear, committed by a tenant. ● A tenant who causes or permits waste is usu. liable to the property owner for damages.

weight of the evidence. The persuasiveness of some evidence in comparison with other evidence <because the verdict is against the great weight of the evidence, a new trial should be granted>. See BURDEN OF PERSUASION.

whistleblower. An employee who reports employer misconduct to a government or law-enforcement agency. ● Federal and state laws protect whistleblowers from employer retaliation.

white-collar crime. A nonviolent crime usu. involving cheating or dishonesty in commercial matters. ● Examples are fraud, bribery, and insider trading.

will, *n.* A document in which a person directs how his or her estate should be distributed upon death.

will contest. In probate law, the litigation of a will's validity, usu. based on allegations that the testator lacked testamentary capacity or was under undue influence when the will was made.

witness, *n.* **1.** One who sees, knows, or vouches for something <a witness to the accident>. **2.** One who gives testimony under oath or affirmation, either orally or by affidavit or deposition <the defense called only one witness>.

workers' compensation. A system of providing benefits to an employee for injuries occurring in the scope of employment. ● Most workers'-compensation statutes hold the employer strictly liable and bar the employee from suing the employer in tort.

writ. A court's written order, in the name of a state or other competent legal authority, commanding the addressee to do or refrain from doing some specified act.

writ of certiorari. See CERTIORARI.

writ of error. An appellate court's written order directing a lower court to deliver the record in the case for review.

writ of habeas corpus. See HABEAS CORPUS.

writ of mandamus. See MANDAMUS.

wrong, *n.* A breach of one's legal duty; a violation of another's legal right.

wrongful-death action. A lawsuit brought on behalf of a decedent's survivors for their damages resulting from a tortious injury that caused the decedent's death. Cf. SURVIVAL ACTION.

XYZ

yellow-dog contract. An employment agreement forbidding membership in a labor union. • Yellow-dog contracts are generally illegal under federal and state statutes.

zone of privacy. In constitutional law, a range of fundamental privacy rights that are implied in the express guarantees of the Bill of Rights. See RIGHT OF PRIVACY.

zoning. The legislative division of a region, esp. a municipality, into separate districts with different regulations within the districts as to land use, building size, and the like.

*

Appendix A

THE CONSTITUTION OF THE UNITED STATES OF AMERICA

We the People of the United States, in Order to form a more perfect Union, establish Justice, insure domestic Tranquility, provide for the common defence, promote the general Welfare, and secure the Blessings of Liberty to ourselves and our Posterity, do ordain and establish this Constitution for the United States of America.

Article I

Section 1. All legislative Powers herein granted shall be vested in a Congress of the United States, which shall consist of a Senate and House of Representatives.

Section 2. The House of Representatives shall be composed of Members chosen every second Year by the People of the several States, and the Electors in each State shall have the Qualifications requisite for Electors of the most numerous Branch of the State Legislature.

No Person shall be a Representative who shall not have attained to the Age of twenty five Years, and been seven Years a Citizen of the United States, and who shall not, when elected, be an Inhabitant of that State in which he shall be chosen.

Representatives and direct Taxes shall be apportioned among the several States which may be included within this Union, according to their respective Numbers, which shall be determined by adding to the whole Number of free Persons, including those bound to Service for a Term of Years, and excluding Indians not taxed, three fifths of all other Persons. The actual Enumeration shall be made within three Years after the first Meeting of the Congress of the United States, and within every subsequent Term of ten Years, in such Manner as they shall by Law direct. The Number of Representatives shall not exceed one for every thirty Thousand, but each State shall have at Least one Representative; and until such enumeration shall be made, the State of New Hampshire shall be entitled to chuse three, Massachusetts eight, Rhode Island and Providence Plantations one, Connecticut five, New York six, New Jersey four, Pennsylvania eight, Delaware one, Maryland six, Virginia ten, North Carolina five, South Carolina five, and Georgia three.

When vacancies happen in the Representation from any State, the Executive Authority thereof shall issue Writs of Election to fill such Vacancies.

The House of Representatives shall chuse their Speaker and other Officers; and shall have the sole Power of Impeachment.

Section 3. The Senate of the United States shall be composed of two Senators from each State, chosen by the Legislature thereof, for six Years; and each Senator shall have one Vote.

Immediately after they shall be assembled in Consequence of the first Election, they shall be divided as equally as may be into three Classes. The Seats of the Senators of the first Class shall be vacated at the Expiration of the Second Year, of the second Class at the Expiration of the fourth Year, and of the third Class at the Expiration of the sixth Year, so that one third may be chosen every second Year; and if Vacancies happen by Resignation, or otherwise, during the Recess of the Legislature of any State, the Executive thereof may make temporary Appointments until the next Meeting of the Legislature, which shall then fill such Vacancies.

No Person shall be a Senator who shall not have attained to the Age of thirty Years, and been nine Years a Citizen of the United States, and who shall not, when elected, be an Inhabitant of that State for which he shall be chosen.

The Vice President of the United States shall be President of the Senate, but shall have no Vote, unless they be equally divided.

The Senate shall chuse their other Officers, and also a President pro tempore, in the Absence of the Vice President, or when he shall exercise the Office of President of the United States.

The Senate shall have the sole Power to try all Impeachments. When sitting for that Purpose, they shall be on Oath or Affirmation. When the President of the United States is tried, the Chief Justice shall preside: And no Person shall be convicted without the Concurrence of two thirds of the Members present.

Judgment in Cases of Impeachment shall not extend further than to removal from Office, and disqualification to hold and enjoy any Office of honor, Trust or Profit under the United States: but the Party convicted shall nevertheless be liable and subject to Indictment, Trial, Judgment and Punishment, according to Law.

Section 4. The Times, Places and Manner of holding Elections for Senators and Representatives, shall be prescribed in each State by the Legislature thereof; but the Congress may at any time by Law make or alter such Regulations, except as to the Places of chusing Senators.

The Congress shall assemble at least once in every Year, and such Meeting shall be on the first Monday in December, unless they shall by Law appoint a different Day.

Section 5. Each House shall be the Judge of the Elections, Returns and Qualifications of its own Members, and a Majority of each shall constitute a Quorum to do Business; but a smaller Number may adjourn from day to day, and may be authorized to compel the Attendance of absent Members, in such Manner, and under such Penalties as each House may provide.

Each House may determine the Rules of its Proceedings, punish its Members for disorderly Behavior, and, with the Concurrence of two thirds, expel a Member.

Each House shall keep a Journal of its Proceedings, and from time to time publish the same, excepting such Parts as may in their Judgment require Secrecy; and the Yeas and Nays of the Members of either House on any question shall, at the Desire of one fifth of those Present, be entered on the Journal.

Neither House, during the Session of Congress, shall, without the Consent of the other, adjourn for more than three days, nor to any other Place than that in which the two Houses shall be sitting.

Section 6. The Senators and Representatives shall receive a Compensation for their Services, to be ascertained by Law, and paid out of the Treasury of the United States. They shall in all Cases, except Treason, Felony and Breach of the Peace, be privileged from Arrest during their Attendance at the Session of their respective Houses, and in going to and returning from the same; and for any Speech or Debate in either House, they shall not be questioned in any other Place.

No Senator or Representative shall, during the Time for which he was elected, be appointed to any civil Office under the Authority of the United States, which shall have been created, or the Emoluments whereof shall have been encreased during such time; and no Person holding any Office under the United States, shall be a Member of either House during his Continuance in Office.

Section 7. All Bills for raising Revenue shall originate in the House of Representatives; but the Senate may propose or concur with Amendments as on other Bills.

Every Bill which shall have passed the House of Representatives and the Senate, shall, before it become a Law, be presented to the President of the United States; If he approve he shall sign it, but if not he shall return it, with his Objections to the House in which it shall have originated, who shall enter the Objections at large on their Journal, and proceed to reconsider it. If after such Reconsideration two thirds of that House shall agree to pass the Bill, it shall be sent, together with the Objections, to the other House, by which it shall likewise be reconsidered, and if approved by two thirds of that House, it shall become a Law. But in all such Cases the Votes of both Houses shall be determined by yeas and Nays, and the Names of the Persons voting for and against the Bill shall be entered on the Journal of each House respectively. If any Bill shall not be returned by the President within ten Days (Sundays excepted) after it shall have been presented to him, the Same shall be a Law, in like Manner as if he had signed it, unless the Congress by their Adjournment prevent its Return, in which Case it shall not be a Law.

Every Order, Resolution, or Vote to which the Concurrence of the Senate and House of Representatives may be necessary (except on a question of Adjournment) shall be presented to the President of the United States; and before the Same shall take Effect, shall be approved by him, or being disapproved by him, shall be repassed by two thirds of the Senate and House of Representatives, according to the Rules and Limitations prescribed in the Case of a Bill.

Section 8. The Congress shall have Power To lay and collect Taxes, Duties, Imposts and Excises, to pay the Debts and provide for the common Defence and general Welfare of the United States; but all Duties, Imposts and Excises shall be uniform throughout the United States;

To borrow Money on the credit of the United States;

To regulate Commerce with foreign Nations, and among the several States, and with the Indian Tribes;

To establish an uniform Rule of Naturalization, and uniform Laws on the subject of Bankruptcies throughout the United States;

To coin Money, regulate the Value thereof, and of foreign Coin, and fix the Standard of Weights and Measures;

To provide for the Punishment of counterfeiting the Securities and current Coin of the United States;

To establish Post Offices and post Roads;

To promote the Progress of Science and useful Arts, by securing for limited Times to Authors and Inventors the exclusive Right to their respective Writings and Discoveries;

To constitute Tribunals inferior to the supreme Court;

To define and punish Piracies and Felonies committed on the high Seas, and Offences against the Law of Nations;

To declare War, grant Letters of Marque and Reprisal, and make Rules concerning Captures on Land and Water;

To raise and support Armies, but no Appropriation of Money to that Use shall be for a longer Term than two Years;

To provide and maintain a Navy;

To make Rules for the Government and Regulation of the land and naval Forces;

To provide for calling forth the Militia to execute the Laws of the Union, suppress Insurrections and repel Invasions;

To provide for organizing, arming, and disciplining, the Militia, and for governing such Part of them as may be employed in the Service of the United States, reserving to the States respectively, the Appointment of the Officers, and the Authority of training the Militia according to the discipline prescribed by Congress;

To exercise exclusive Legislation in all Cases whatsoever, over such District (not exceeding ten Miles square) as may, by Cession of particular States, and the Acceptance of Congress, become the Seat of the Government of the United States, and to exercise like Authority over all Places purchased by the Consent of the Legislature of the State in which the Same shall be, for the Erection of Forts, Magazines, Arsenals, dock-Yards, and other needful Buildings;—And

To make all Laws which shall be necessary and proper for carrying into Execution the foregoing Powers, and all other Powers vested by this Constitution in the Government of the United States, or in any Department or Officer thereof.

Section 9. The Migration or Importation of Such Persons as any of the States now existing shall think proper to admit, shall not be prohibited by the Congress prior to the Year one thousand eight hundred and eight, but a Tax or duty may be imposed on such Importation, not exceeding ten dollars for each Person.

The Privilege of the Writ of Habeas Corpus shall not be suspended, unless when in Cases of Rebellion or Invasion the public Safety may require it.

No Bill of Attainder or ex post facto Law shall be passed.

No Capitation, or other direct, Tax shall be laid, unless in Proportion to the Census or Enumeration herein before directed to be taken.

No Tax or Duty shall be laid on Articles exported from any State.

No Preference shall be given by any Regulation of Commerce or Revenue to the Ports of one State over those of another: nor shall Vessels bound to, or from, one State, be obliged to enter, clear, or pay Duties in another.

No Money shall be drawn from the Treasury, but in Consequence of Appropriations made by Law; and a regular Statement and Account of the Receipts and Expenditures of all public Money shall be published from time to time.

No Title of Nobility shall be granted by the United States: And no Person holding any Office of Profit or Trust under them, shall, without the Consent of the Congress, accept of any present, Emolument, Office, or Title, of any kind whatever, from any King, Prince, or foreign State.

Section 10. No State shall enter into any Treaty, Alliance, or Confederation; grant Letters of Marque and Reprisal; coin Money; emit Bills of Credit; make any Thing but gold and silver Coin a Tender in Payment of Debts;

pass any Bill of Attainder, ex post facto Law, or Law impairing the Obligation of Contracts, or grant any Title of Nobility.

No State shall, without the Consent of the Congress, lay any Imposts or Duties on Imports or Exports, except what may be absolutely necessary for executing its inspection Laws: and the net Produce of all Duties and Imposts, laid by any State on Imports or Exports, shall be for the Use of the Treasury of the United States; and all such Laws shall be subject to the Revision and Controul of the Congress.

No State shall, without the Consent of Congress, lay any Duty of Tonnage, keep Troops, or Ships of War in time of Peace, enter into any Agreement or Compact with another State, or with a foreign Power, or engage in War, unless actually invaded, or in such imminent Danger as will not admit of delay.

Article II

Section 1. The executive Power shall be vested in a President of the United States of America. He shall hold his Office during the Term of four Years, and, together with the Vice President, chosen for the same Term, be elected, as follows:

Each State shall appoint, in such Manner as the Legislature thereof may direct, a Number of Electors, equal to the whole Number of Senators and Representatives to which the State may be entitled in the Congress: but no Senator or Representative, or Person holding an Office of Trust or Profit under the United States, shall be appointed an Elector.

The Electors shall meet in their respective States, and vote by Ballot for two Persons, of whom one at least shall not be an Inhabitant of the same State with themselves. And they shall make a List of all the Persons voted for, and of the Number of Votes for each; which List they shall sign and certify, and transmit sealed to the Seat of the Government of the United States, directed to the President of the Senate. The President of the Senate shall, in the Presence of the Senate and House of Representatives, open all the Certificates, and the Votes shall then be counted. The Person having the greatest Number of Votes shall be the President, if such Number be a Majority of the whole Number of Electors appointed; and if there be more than one who have such Majority, and have an equal Number of Votes, then the House of Representatives shall immediately chuse by Ballot one of them for President; and if no Person have a Majority, then from the five highest on the List the said House shall in like Manner chuse the President. But in chusing the President, the Votes shall be taken by States, the Representation from each State having one Vote; A quorum for this Purpose shall consist of a Member or Members from two thirds of the States, and a Majority of all the States shall be necessary to a Choice. In every Case, after the Choice of the President, the Person having the greater Number of Votes of the Electors shall be the Vice President. But if there should remain two or more who have equal Votes, the Senate shall chuse from them by Ballot the Vice President.

The Congress may determine the Time of chusing the Electors, and the Day on which they shall give their Votes; which Day shall be the same throughout the United States.

No Person except a natural born Citizen, or a Citizen of the United States, at the time of the Adoption of this Constitution, shall be eligible to the Office of President; neither shall any Person be eligible to that Office who shall not have attained to the Age of thirty five Years, and been fourteen Years a Resident within the United States.

In Case of the Removal of the President from Office, or of his Death, Resignation or Inability to discharge the Powers and Duties of the said Office, the Same shall devolve on the Vice President and the Congress may by Law provide for the Case of Removal, Death, Resignation or Inability, both of the President and Vice President, declaring what Officer shall then act as President, and such Officer shall act accordingly, until the Disability be removed, or a President shall be elected.

The President shall, at stated Times, receive for his Services, a Compensation, which shall neither be increased nor diminished during the Period for which he shall have been elected, and he shall not receive within that Period any other Emolument from the United States, or any of them.

Before he enter on the Execution of his Office, he shall take the following Oath or Affirmation: "I do solemnly swear (or affirm) that I will faithfully execute the Office of President of the United States, and will to the best of my Ability, preserve, protect and defend the Constitution of the United States."

Section 2. The President shall be Commander in Chief of the Army and Navy of the United States, and of the Militia of the several States, when called into the actual Service of the United States; he may require the Opinion, in writing, of the principal Officer in each of the Executive Departments, upon any Subject relating to the Duties of their respective Offices and he shall have Power to grant Reprieves and Pardons for Offences against the United States, except in Cases of Impeachment.

He shall have Power, by and with the Advice and Consent of the Senate, to make Treaties, provided two thirds of the Senators present concur; and he shall nominate, and by and with the Advice and Consent of the

Senate, shall appoint Ambassadors, other public Ministers and Consuls, Judges of the supreme Court, and all other Officers of the United States, whose Appointments are not herein otherwise provided for, and which shall be established by Law: but the Congress may by Law vest the Appointment of such inferior Officers, as they think proper, in the President alone, in the Courts of Law, or in the Heads of Departments.

The President shall have Power to fill up all Vacancies that may happen during the Recess of the Senate, by granting Commissions which shall expire at the End of their next Session.

Section 3. He shall from time to time give to the Congress Information of the State of the Union, and recommend to their Consideration such Measures as he shall judge necessary and expedient; he may, on extraordinary Occasions, convene both Houses, or either of them, and in Case of Disagreement between them, with Respect to the Time of Adjournment, he may adjourn them to such Time as he shall think proper; he shall receive Ambassadors and other public Ministers; he shall take Care that the Laws be faithfully executed, and shall Commission all the Officers of the United States.

Section 4. The President, Vice President and all civil Officers of the United States, shall be removed from Office on Impeachment for, and Conviction of, Treason, Bribery, or other high Crimes and Misdemeanors.

Article III

Section 1. The judicial Power of the United States, shall be vested in one supreme Court, and in such inferior Courts as the Congress may from time to time ordain and establish. The Judges, both of the supreme and inferior Courts, shall hold their Offices during good Behaviour, and shall, at stated Times, receive for their Services a Compensation, which shall not be diminished during their Continuance in Office.

Section 2. The judicial Power shall extend to all Cases, in Law and Equity, arising under this Constitution, the Laws of the United States, and Treaties made, or which shall be made, under their Authority;—to all Cases affecting Ambassadors, other public Ministers and Consuls;—to all Cases of admiralty and maritime Jurisdiction;—to Controversies to which the United States shall be a Party;—to Controversies between two or more States;—between a State and Citizens of another State;—between Citizens of different States;—between Citizens of the same State claiming Lands under the Grants of different States, and between a State, or the Citizens thereof, and foreign States, Citizens or Subjects.

In all Cases affecting Ambassadors, other public Ministers and Consuls, and those in which a State shall be a Party, the supreme Court shall have original Jurisdiction. In all the other Cases before mentioned, the supreme Court shall have appellate Jurisdiction, both as to Law and Fact, with such Exceptions, and under such Regulations as the Congress shall make.

The trial of all Crimes, except in Cases of Impeachment, shall be by Jury; and such Trial shall be held in the State where the said Crimes shall have been committed; but when not committed within any State, the Trial shall be at such Place or Places as the Congress may by Law have directed.

Section 3. Treason against the United States, shall consist only in levying War against them, or, in adhering to their Enemies, giving them Aid and Comfort. No Person shall be convicted of Treason unless on the Testimony of two Witnesses to the same overt Act, or on Confession in open Court.

The Congress shall have Power to declare the Punishment of Treason, but no Attainder of Treason shall work Corruption of Blood, or Forfeiture except during the Life of the Person attainted.

Article IV

Section 1. Full Faith and Credit shall be given in each State to the public Acts, Records, and judicial Proceedings of every other State. And the Congress may by general Laws prescribe the Manner in which such Acts, Records and Proceedings shall be proved, and the Effect thereof.

Section 2. The Citizens of each State shall be entitled to all Privileges and Immunities of Citizens in the several States.

A Person charged in any State with Treason, Felony, or other Crime, who shall flee from Justice, and be found in another State, shall on demand of the executive Authority of the State from which he fled, be delivered up, to be removed to the State having Jurisdiction of the Crime.

No Person held to Service or Labour in one State, under the Laws thereof, escaping into another, shall, in Consequence of any Law or Regulation therein, be discharged from such Service or Labour, but shall be delivered up on Claim of the Party to whom such Service or Labour may be due.

Section 3. New States may be admitted by the Congress into this Union; but no new State shall be formed or erected with the Jurisdiction of any other State; nor any State be formed by the Junction of two or more States, or Parts of States, without the Consent of the Legislatures of the States concerned as well as of the Congress.

The Congress shall have Power to dispose of and make all needful Rules and Regulations respecting the Territory or other Property belonging to the United States; and nothing in this Constitution shall be so construed as to Prejudice any Claims of the United States, or of any particular State.

Section 4. The United States shall guarantee to every State in this Union a Republican Form of Government, and shall protect each of them against Invasion; and on Application of the Legislature, or of the Executive (when the Legislature cannot be convened) against domestic Violence.

Article V

The Congress, whenever two thirds of both Houses shall deem it necessary, shall propose Amendments to this Constitution, or, on the Application of the Legislatures of two thirds of the several States, shall call a Convention for proposing Amendments, which, in either Case, shall be valid to all Intents and Purposes, as Part of this Constitution, when ratified by the Legislatures of three fourths of the several States, or by Conventions in three fourths thereof, as the one or the other Mode of Ratification may be proposed by the Congress; Provided that no Amendment which may be made prior to the Year One thousand eight hundred and eight shall in any Manner affect the first and fourth Clauses in the Ninth Section of the first Article; and that no State, without its Consent, shall be deprived of its equal Suffrage in the Senate.

Article VI

All Debts contracted and Engagements entered into, before the Adoption of this Constitution, shall be as valid against the United States under this Constitution, as under the Confederation.

This Constitution, and the Laws of the United States which shall be made in Pursuance thereof; and all Treaties made, or which shall be made, under the Authority of the United States, shall be the supreme Law of the Land; and the Judges in every State shall be bound thereby, any Thing in the Constitution or Laws of any State to the Contrary notwithstanding.

The Senators and Representatives before mentioned, and the Members of the several State Legislatures, and all executive and judicial Officers, both of the United States and of the several States, shall be bound by Oath or Affirmation, to support this Constitution; but no religious Test shall ever be required as a Qualification to any Office or public Trust under the United States.

Article VII

The Ratification of the Conventions of nine States, shall be sufficient for the Establishment of this Constitution between the States so ratifying the Same.

ARTICLES IN ADDITION TO, AND AMENDMENT OF, THE CONSTITUTION OF THE UNITED STATES OF AMERICA, PROPOSED BY CONGRESS, AND RATIFIED BY THE LEGISLATURES OF THE SEVERAL STATES PURSUANT TO THE FIFTH ARTICLE OF THE ORIGINAL CONSTITUTION.

Amendment I [1791]

Congress shall make no law respecting an establishment of religion, or prohibiting the free exercise thereof; or abridging the freedom of speech, or of the press; or the right of the people peaceably to assemble, and to petition the Government for a redress of grievances.

Amendment II [1791]

A well regulated Militia, being necessary to the security of a free State, the right of the people to keep and bear Arms, shall not be infringed.

Amendment III [1791]

No Soldier shall, in time of peace be quartered in any house, without the consent of the Owner, nor in time of war, but in a manner to be prescribed by law.

Amendment IV [1791]

The right of the people to be secure in their persons, houses, papers, and effects, against unreasonable searches and seizures, shall not be violated, and no Warrants shall issue, but upon probable cause, supported by Oath or affirmation, and particularly describing the place to be searched, and the persons or things to be seized.

Amendment V [1791]

No person shall be held to answer for a capital, or otherwise infamous crime, unless on a presentment or indictment of a Grand Jury, except in cases arising in the land or naval forces, or in the Militia, when in actual service in time of War or public danger; nor shall any person be subject for the same offence to be twice put in jeopardy of life or limb; nor shall be compelled in any criminal case to be a witness against himself, nor be deprived of life, liberty, or property, without due process of law; nor shall private property be taken for public use, without just compensation.

Amendment VI [1791]

In all criminal prosecutions, the accused shall enjoy the right to a speedy and public trial, by an impartial jury of the State and district wherein the crime shall have been committed, which district shall have been previously ascertained by law, and to be informed of the nature and cause of the accusation; to be confronted with the witnesses against him; to have compulsory process for obtaining witnesses in his favor, and to have the Assistance of Counsel for his defence.

Amendment VII [1791]

In Suits at common law, where the value in controversy shall exceed twenty dollars, the right of trial by jury shall be preserved, and no fact tried by jury, shall be otherwise re-examined in any Court of the United States, than according to the rules of the common law.

Amendment VIII [1791]

Excessive bail shall not be required, nor excessive fines imposed, nor cruel and unusual punishments inflicted.

Amendment IX [1791]

The enumeration in the Constitution, of certain rights, shall not be construed to deny or disparage others retained by the people.

Amendment X [1791]

The powers not delegated to the United States by the Constitution, nor prohibited by it to the States, are reserved to the States respectively, or to the people.

Amendment XI [1798]

The Judicial power of the United States shall not be construed to extend to any suit in law or equity, commenced or prosecuted against one of the United States by

Citizens of another State, or by Citizens or Subjects of any Foreign State.

Amendment XII [1804]

The Electors shall meet in their respective states and vote by ballot for President and Vice-President, one of whom, at least, shall not be an inhabitant of the same state with themselves; they shall name in their ballots the person voted for as President, and in distinct ballots the person voted for as Vice-President, and they shall make distinct lists of all persons voted for as President, and of all persons voted for as Vice-President, and of the number of votes for each, which lists they shall sign and certify, and transmit sealed to the seat of the government of the United States, directed to the President of the Senate;— The President of the Senate shall, in the presence of the Senate and House of Representatives, open all the certificates and the votes shall then be counted;—The person having the greatest number of votes for President, shall be the President, if such number be a majority of the whole number of Electors appointed; and if no person have such majority, then from the persons having the highest numbers not exceeding three on the list of those voted for as President, the House of Representatives shall choose immediately, by ballot, the President. But in choosing the President, the votes shall be taken by states, the representation from each state having one vote; a quorum for this purpose shall consist of a member or members from two-thirds of the states, and a majority of all the states shall be necessary to a choice. And if the House of Representatives shall not choose a President whenever the right of choice shall devolve upon them before the fourth day of March next following, then the Vice-President shall act as President, as in the case of the death or other constitutional disability of the President.—The person having the greatest number of votes as Vice-President, shall be the Vice-President, if such number be a majority of the whole number of Electors appointed, and if no person have a majority, then from the two highest numbers on the list, the Senate shall choose the Vice-President; a quorum for the purpose shall consist of two-thirds of the whole number of Senators, and a majority of the whole number shall be necessary to a choice. But no person constitutionally ineligible to the office of President shall be eligible to that of Vice-President of the United States.

Amendment XIII [1865]

Section 1. Neither slavery nor involuntary servitude, except as a punishment for crime whereof the party shall have been duly convicted, shall exist within the United States, or any place subject to their jurisdiction.

Section 2. Congress shall have power to enforce this article by appropriate legislation.

Amendment XIV [1868]

Section 1. All persons born or naturalized in the United States, and subject to the jurisdiction thereof, are citizens of the United States and of the State wherein they reside. No State shall make or enforce any law which shall abridge the privileges or immunities of citizens of the United States; nor shall any State deprive any person of life, liberty, or property, without due process of law; nor deny to any person within its jurisdiction the equal protection of the laws.

Section 2. Representatives shall be apportioned among the several States according to their respective numbers, counting the whole number of persons in each State, excluding Indians not taxed. But when the right to vote at any election for the choice of electors for President and

Vice President of the United States, Representatives in Congress, the Executive and Judicial officers of a State, or the members of the Legislature thereof, is denied to any of the male inhabitants of such State, being twenty-one years of age, and citizens of the United States, or in any way abridged, except for participation in rebellion, or other crime, the basis of representation therein shall be reduced in the proportion which the number of such male citizens shall bear to the whole number of male citizens twenty-one years of age in such State.

Section 3. No person shall be a Senator or Representative in Congress, or elector of President and Vice President, or hold any office, civil or military, under the United States, or under any State, who, having previously taken an oath, as a member of Congress, or as an officer of the United States, or as a member of any State legislature, or as an executive or judicial officer of any State, to support the Constitution of the United States, shall have engaged in insurrection or rebellion against the same, or given aid or comfort to the enemies thereof. But Congress may by a vote of two-thirds of each House, remove such disability.

Section 4. The validity of the public debt of the United States, authorized by law, including debts incurred for payment of pensions and bounties for services in suppressing insurrection or rebellion, shall not be questioned. But neither the United States nor any State shall assume or pay any debt or obligation incurred in aid of insurrection or rebellion against the United States, or any claim for the loss or emancipation of any slave; but all such debts, obligations and claims shall be held illegal and void.

Section 5. The Congress shall have power to enforce, by appropriate legislation, the provisions of this article.

Amendment XV [1870]

Section 1. The right of citizens of the United States to vote shall not be denied or abridged by the United States or by any State on account of race, color, or previous condition of servitude.

Section 2. The Congress shall have power to enforce this article by appropriate legislation.

Amendment XVI [1913]

The Congress shall have power to lay and collect taxes on incomes, from whatever source derived, without apportionment among the several States, and without regard to any census or enumeration.

Amendment XVII [1913]

[1] The Senate of the United States shall be composed of two Senators from each State, elected by the people thereof, for six years; and each Senator shall have one vote. The electors in each State shall have the qualifications requisite for electors of the most numerous branch of the State legislatures.

[2] When vacancies happen in the representation of any State in the Senate, the executive authority of such State shall issue writs of election to fill such vacancies: *Provided,* That the legislature of any State may empower the executive thereof to make temporary appointments until the people fill the vacancies by election as the legislature may direct.

[3] This amendment shall not be so construed as to affect the election or term of any Senator chosen before it becomes valid as part of the Constitution.

Amendment XVIII [1919]

Section 1. After one year from the ratification of this article the manufacture, sale, or transportation of intoxicating liquors within, the importation thereof into, or the exportation thereof from the United States and all territory subject to the jurisdiction thereof for beverage purposes is hereby prohibited.

Section 2. The Congress and the several States shall have concurrent power to enforce this article by appropriate legislation.

Section 3. This article shall be inoperative unless it shall have been ratified as an amendment to the Constitution by the legislatures of the several States, as provided in the Constitution, within seven years from the date of the submission hereof to the States by the Congress.

Amendment XIX [1920]

[1] The right of citizens of the United States to vote shall not be denied or abridged by the United States or by any State on account of sex.

[2] Congress shall have power to enforce this article by appropriate legislation.

Amendment XX [1933]

Section 1. The terms of the President and Vice President shall end at noon on the 20th day of January, and the terms of Senators and Representatives at noon on the 3d day of January, of the years in which such terms would have ended if this article had not been ratified; and the terms of their successors shall then begin.

Section 2. The Congress shall assemble at least once in every year, and such meeting shall begin at noon on the 3d day of January, unless they shall by law appoint a different day.

Section 3. If, at the time fixed for the beginning of the term of the President, the President elect shall have died, the Vice President elect shall become President. If the

President shall not have been chosen before the time fixed for the beginning of his term, or if the President elect shall have failed to qualify, then the Vice President elect shall act as President until a President shall have qualified; and the Congress may by law provide for the case wherein neither a President elect nor a Vice President elect shall have qualified, declaring who shall then act as President, or the manner in which one who is to act shall be selected, and such person shall act accordingly until a President or Vice President shall have qualified.

Section 4. The Congress may by law provide for the case of the death of any of the persons from whom the House of Representatives may choose a President whenever the right of choice shall have devolved upon them, and for the case of the death of any of the persons from whom the Senate may choose a Vice President whenever the right of choice shall have devolved upon them.

Section 5. Sections 1 and 2 shall take effect on the 15th day of October following the ratification of this article.

Section 6. This article shall be inoperative unless it shall have been ratified as an amendment to the Constitution by the legislatures of three-fourths of the several States within seven years from the date of its submission.

Amendment XXI [1933]

Section 1. The eighteenth article of amendment to the Constitution of the United States is hereby repealed.

Section 2. The transportation or importation into any State, Territory, or possession of the United States for delivery or use therein of intoxicating liquors, in violation of the laws thereof, is hereby prohibited.

Section 3. This article shall be inoperative unless it shall have been ratified as an amendment to the Constitution by conventions in the several States, as provided in the Constitution, within seven years from the date of the submission hereof to the States by the Congress.

Amendment XXII [1951]

Section 1. No person shall be elected to the office of the President more than twice, and no person who has held the office of President, or acted as President, for more than two years of a term to which some other person was elected President shall be elected to the office of President more than once. But this Article shall not apply to any person holding the office of President when this Article was proposed by the Congress, and shall not prevent any person who may be holding the office of President, or acting as President, during the term within which this Article becomes operative from holding the office of President or acting as President during the remainder of such term.

Section 2. This article shall be inoperative unless it shall have been ratified as an amendment to the Constitution by the legislatures of three-fourths of the several States within seven years from the date of its submission to the States by the Congress.

Amendment XXIII [1961]

Section 1. The District constituting the seat of Government of the United States shall appoint in such manner as the Congress may direct:

A number of electors of President and Vice President equal to the whole number of Senators and Representatives in Congress to which the District would be entitled if it were a State, but in no event more than the least populous state; they shall be in addition to those appointed by the states, but they shall be considered, for the purposes of the election of President and Vice President, to be electors appointed by a state; and they shall meet in the District and perform such duties as provided by the twelfth article of amendment.

Section 2. The Congress shall have power to enforce this article by appropriate legislation.

Amendment XXIV [1964]

Section 1. The right of citizens of the United States to vote in any primary or other election for President or Vice President, for electors for President or Vice President, or for Senator or Representative in Congress, shall not be denied or abridged by the United States or any State by reason of failure to pay any poll tax or other tax.

Section 2. The Congress shall have power to enforce this article by appropriate legislation.

Amendment XXV [1967]

Section 1. In the case of the removal of the President from office or of his death or resignation, the Vice President shall become President.

Section 2. Whenever there is a vacancy in the office of the Vice President, the President shall nominate a Vice President who shall take office upon confirmation by a majority vote of both Houses of Congress.

Section 3. Whenever the President transmits to the President pro tempore of the Senate and the Speaker of the House of Representatives his written declaration that he is unable to discharge the powers and duties of his office, and until he transmits to them a written declaration to the contrary, such powers and duties shall be discharged by the Vice President as Acting President.

Section 4. Whenever the Vice President and a majority of either the principal officers of the executive departments or of such other body as Congress may by law provide, transmit to the President pro tempore of the Senate and the Speaker of the House of Representatives their written declaration that the President is unable to discharge the powers and duties of his office, the Vice President shall immediately assume the powers and duties of the office as Acting President.

Thereafter, when the President transmits to the President pro tempore of the Senate and the Speaker of the House of Representatives his written declaration that no inability exists, he shall resume the powers and duties of his office unless the Vice President and a majority of either the principal officers of the executive department or of such other body as Congress may by law provide, transmit within four days to the President pro tempore of the Senate and the Speaker of the House of Representatives their written declaration that the President is unable to discharge the powers and duties of his office. Thereupon Congress shall decide the issue, assembling within forty-eight hours for that purpose if not in session. If the Congress, within twenty-one days after receipt of the latter written declaration, or, if Congress is not in session, within twenty-one days after Congress is required to assemble, determines by two-thirds vote of both Houses that the President is unable to discharge the powers and duties of his office, the Vice President shall continue to discharge the same as Acting President; otherwise, the President shall resume the powers and duties of his office.

Amendment XXVI [1971]

Section 1. The right of citizens of the United States, who are eighteen years of age or older, to vote shall not be denied or abridged by the United States or by any State on account of age.

Section 2. The Congress shall have power to enforce this article by appropriate legislation.

Amendment XXVII [1992]

No Law, varying the compensation for the services of the Senators and Representatives, shall take effect, until an election of Representatives shall have intervened.

Appendix B

LEGAL WORDBOOKS

Black's Law Dictionary. 6th ed. St. Paul, Minn.: West, 1990.

Clapp, James E. *Random House Legal Dictionary*. N.Y.: Random House, 1996.

Garner, Bryan A. *A Dictionary of Modern Legal Usage*. 2d ed. N.Y.: Oxford Univ. Press, 1995.

Garner, Bryan A., ed. *Black's Law Dictionary*. Pocket ed. St. Paul, Minn.: West, 1996.

Merriam–Webster's Dictionary of Law. Springfield, Mass.: Merriam–Webster, 1996.

Walker, David M. *The Oxford Companion to Law*. Oxford: Oxford Univ. Press, 1980.

Words and Phrases. 90 vols. and supps. St. Paul, Minn.: West, 1940–1998.

*

Appendix C

INTRODUCTORY BOOKS ON LAW

American Bar Association. *You and the Law*. Lincolnwood, Ill.: Publications Int'l, 1990.

Friedman, Lawrence. *American Law: An Introduction*. Rev. ed. N.Y.: W.W. Norton & Co., 1998.

Hegland, Kenney. *Introduction to the Study and Practice of Law*. 2d ed. St. Paul, Minn.: West, 1995.

Irving, Shae, ed. *Nolo's Everyday Law Book*. Berkeley, Cal.: Nolo Press, 1996.

Kempin, Frederick G. *Historical Introduction to Anglo-American Law in a Nutshell*. 3d ed. St. Paul, Minn.: West, 1990.

Reader's Digest Legal Problem Solver: A Quick-and-Easy Action Guide to the Law. Pleasantville, N.Y.: Reader's Digest, 1994.

Sack, Steven Michael. *The Lifetime Legal Guide*. N.Y.: Book-of-the-Month Club, 1996.

*

Appendix D

BASIC LAWBOOKS

Bankruptcy

Epstein, David G. *Bankruptcy and Other Debtor-Creditor Laws in a Nutshell*. 5th ed. St. Paul, Minn.: West, 1995.

Business Law

Hamilton, Robert W. *Fundamentals of Modern Business*. Boston: Little, Brown & Co., 1989.

Hardwicke, John W.; and Robert W. Emerson. *Business Law*. N.Y.: Barron's, 1997.

Henn, Harry G.; and John R. Alexander. *Laws of Corporations and Other Business Enterprises*. 3d ed. St. Paul, Minn.: West, 1996.

Constitutional Law

Hall, Kermit L. *The Oxford Companion to the Supreme Court of the United States*. N.Y.: Oxford Univ. Press, 1992.

Lieberman, Jethro K. *The Evolving Constitution*. N.Y.: Random House, 1992.

Nowak, John E.; and Ronald D. Rotunda. *Constitutional Law*. 5th ed. St. Paul, Minn.: West, 1995.

Tribe, Laurence H. *American Constitutional Law*. Mineola, N.Y.: Foundation Press, 1978.

Contracts

Calamari, John D.; and Joseph M. Perillo. *Contracts*. 4th ed. St. Paul, Minn.: West, 1998.

Farnsworth, E. Allan. *Contracts*. 3d ed. Boston: Little, Brown & Co., 1998.

Rohwer, Claude D.; and Gordon G. Schaber. *Contracts in a Nutshell*. 4th ed. St. Paul, Minn.: West, 1997.

BASIC LAWBOOKS

Criminal Law

LaFave, Wayne R.; and Austin W. Scott. *Criminal Law*. 2d ed. St. Paul, Minn.: West, 1986.

Loewy, Arnold H. *Criminal Law in a Nutshell*. 2d ed. St. Paul, Minn.: West, 1987.

Perkins, Rollin M.; and Ronald N. Boyce. *Criminal Law*. 3d ed. Mineola, N.Y.: Foundation Press, 1982.

Evidence

Park, Roger C.; David P. Leonard; and Steven H. Goldberg. Evidence Law: A Student's Guide to the Law of Evidence as Applied in American Trials. St. Paul, Minn.: West, 1998.

Rothstein, Paul F.; Myrna S. Raeder; and David Crump. *Evidence: State and Federal Rules*. 3d ed. St. Paul, Minn.: West, 1997.

Family Law

Krause, Harry D. *Family Law in a Nutshell*. St. Paul, Minn.: West, 1995.

Leonard, Robin; and Stephen Elias. *Nolo's Pocket Guide to Family Law*. 4th ed. Berkeley, Cal.: Nolo Press, 1996.

Legal Research

Cohen, Morris L.; and Kent C. Olsen. *Legal Research in a Nutshell*. St. Paul, Minn.: West, 1996.

Jacobstein, Myron; and Roy M. Mersky. *Fundamentals of Legal Research*. Mineola, N.Y.: Foundation Press, 1998.

Legal Writing

Garner, Bryan A. *The Elements of Legal Style*. N.Y.: Oxford Univ. Press, 1991.

Good, C. Edward. *Mightier Than the Sword: Powerful Writing in the Legal Profession*. Charlottesville, Va.: Blue Jeans Press, 1989.

Wydick, Richard. *Plain English for Lawyers*. 4th ed. Durham, N.C.: Carolina Academic Press, 1998.

Procedure

Friedenthal, Jack H.; Mary Kay Kane; and Arthur R. Miller. *Civil Procedure*. 2d ed. St. Paul, Minn.: West, 1993.

LaFave, Wayne R.; and Jerold H. Israel. *Criminal Procedure*. 2d ed. St. Paul, Minn.: West, 1992.

Wright, Charles Alan. *Law of Federal Courts*. 5th ed. St. Paul, Minn.: West, 1994.

Property

Boyer, Ralph E.; Herbert Hovenkamp; and Sheldon F. Kurtz. 4th ed. *The Law of Property: An Introductory Survey*. St. Paul, Minn.: West, 1991.

Burke, Barlow. *Personal Property in a Nutshell*. 2d ed. St. Paul, Minn.: West, 1993.

Cunningham, Roger A.; William B. Stoebuck; and Dale A. Whitman. *The Law of Property*. 2d ed. St. Paul, Minn.: West, 1993.

Tax

McNulty, John K. *Federal Estate and Gift Taxation in a Nutshell*. 5th ed. St. Paul, Minn.: West, 1994.

Morgan, Patricia T. *Tax Procedure and Tax Fraud in a Nutshell*. 2nd ed. St. Paul, Minn.: West, 1999.

Torts

Keeton, W. Page, ed. *Prosser and Keeton on Torts*. 5th ed. St. Paul, Minn.: West, 1984.

Kionka, Edward J. *Torts in a Nutshell*. 2d ed. St. Paul, Minn.: West, 1992.

Wills and Estate Planning

Lynn, Robert J. *Introduction to Estate Planning in a Nutshell*. 4th ed. St. Paul, Minn.: West, 1992.

McGovern, William M., Jr.; Sheldon F. Kurtz; and Jan Ellen Rein. *Wills, Trusts, and Estates*. St. Paul, Minn.: West, 1988.

Mennell, Robert L. *Wills and Trusts in a Nutshell*. 2d ed. St. Paul, Minn.: West, 1994.

†